One
Dross is understood as a
natural component of every
dynamically evolving city.
As such it is an indicator of
healthy urban growth.

Two
Drosscapes accumulate in the wake of the socio- and spatio-economic processes of deindustrialization, post-Fordism, and technological innovation.

Three
Drosscapes require the designer to shift thinking from tacit and explicit knowledge (designer as sole expert and authority) to complex interactive and responsive processing (designer as collaborator and negotiator).

Four
The designer does not rely
on the client-consultant
relationship or the contractual
agreement to begin work.
In many cases a client may
not even exist but will
need to be searched out and
custom-fit in order to match
the designer's research
discoveries. In this way the
designer is the consummate
spokesperson for the
productive integration of waste
landscape in the urban world.

Five
Drosscapes are interstitial.
The designer integrates waste
landscapes left over from any
form or type of development.

Six
The adaptability and occupation
of drosscapes depend
upon qualities associated
with decontamination, health,
safety, and reprogramming.
The designer must act, at
times, as the conductor and
at times the agent of these
effects in order to slow down
or speed them up.

Seven
Drosscapes may be unsightly.
There is little concern for
contextual precedence, and
resources are scarce for the
complete scenic amelioration
of drosscapes that are located
in the declining, neglected,
and deindustrializing areas
of cities.

Eight
Drosscapes may be visually pleasing. Wasteful landscapes are purposefully built within all types of new development located on the leading, peripheral edges of urbanization. The designer must discern which types of "waste" may be productively reintegrated for higher social, cultural, and environmental benefits.

Drosscape

Wasting Land in Urban America
Alan Berger

Princeton Architectural Press
New York

Dedication
To Elaine Harris Reiter,
who sees beauty in all the world's dross

Published by
Princeton Architectural Press
37 East Seventh Street
New York, New York 10003

For a free catalog of books, call 1.800.722.6657.
Visit our web site at www.papress.com.

© 2006 Princeton Architectural Press
All rights reserved
Printed and bound in China
10 09 08 07 5 4 3 2 1 First paperback edition

Editing
Jennifer N. Thompson

Cover and book design
Project Projects

Editorial assistance
Lauren Neefe and Lauren Nelson

The photographs and mappings in this book are by the author.
Cover: Phoenix, Arizona

This book has been generously supported by the A. Alfred Taubman
Center for State and Local Government at Harvard's Kennedy School
of Government and Harvard University Center for the Environment.

Special thanks to
Nettie Aljian, Dorothy Ball, Nicola Bednarek, Janet Behning, Becca
Casbon, Penny (Yuen Pik) Chu, Russell Fernandez, Jan Haux, Clare
Jacobson, Mark Lamster, Nancy Eklund Later, Linda Lee, Katharine
Myers, Jane Sheinman, Scott Tennent, Paul Wagner, Joseph Weston, and
Deb Wood of Princeton Architectural Press–Kevin C. Lippert, publisher

ISBN: 978-1-56898-713-2

The Library of Congress has cataloged the hardcover edition of
this book as:
Berger, Alan, 1964-
    Drosscape : wasting land in urban America / Alan Berger ; with a
    postscript by Lars Lerup.–1st ed.
        p. cm.
    Includes bibliographical references and index.
    ISBN 1-56898-572-X (hardcover : alk. paper)
1. City planning–United States. 2. Regional planning–United States.
3. Land use, Urban–United States. 4. Waste lands–United States.
5. Vacant lands–United States. I. Title.
    HT167.B467 2005
    307.1'2160973–dc22
                            2005026156

Preface

As daily life teaches, Murphy's law reminds us, and
the second law of thermodynamics formalizes, nature
produces waste as it grows. Grappling with this fact
design-wise is a fascinating challenge. Landscape
architecture tends to dwell on the traditional areas
of landscape history—site engineering, construction
detailing, and project-based design studio education. But
beyond and behind these topics is an issue so huge we
tend not to see it at all—what I call the drosscape, which
implies that dross, or waste, is "scaped," or resurfaced,
and reprogrammed for adaptive reuse. In this rubric
one may describe drosscaping as a sort of scavenging
of the regional urbanized surface for interstitial
landscape remains. Drosscapes are the inevitable
wasted landscapes within urbanized areas that eternally
elude the overly controlled parameters and the scripted
programming elements that designers are charged
with creating and accommodating in their projects.
Drosscape: Wasting Land in Urban America formally
documents and attempts to develop a new aesthetic
and vocabulary cognizant of this vast, hitherto largely
ignored, field of waste landscapes existing and forming
within America's old and new urbanized regions.

Dross emerges out of two primary processes:
first, as a consequence of current rapid horizontal
urbanization (or what some refer to as urban "sprawl"),
and second, as the leftovers of previous economic
and production regimes, which are both catalyzed
by the drastic decrease in transportation costs (for
goods and people) over the past century.[1] From its
deindustrializing inner core to its sprawling periphery
to the transitional landscapes in between, the city
is the manifestation of industrial processes such as
manufacturing, transporting goods and services, and
natural resource consumption. *Drosscape* investigates
the entire urbanized region as a waste product formed
by and linked to economic and industrial processes.
Its purpose is to understand regional urban landscape
formation, created by the imminent deindustrialization
of older city areas (the downtown core) and the rapid
urbanization of newer city areas (the periphery). It is
an organic phenomenon heedless of the academic
and human boundaries that separate environmental
and architectural/planning/design issues, urban from
suburban issues, and nostalgic definitions of community
from actual organizations of people, workplaces, and
social structures. The basic precept of *Drosscape* is
that planned and unplanned horizontalizations around
vertical urban centers are neither intrinsically bad nor
good but a natural result of industrial growth. These
results require new conceptualization and considered

[1] Edward L. Glaeser and Janet E. Kohlhase, "Cities, Regions and the
Decline of Transport Costs," Harvard Institute of Economic Research,
discussion paper 2014 (Cambridge: Harvard University, July 2003),
http://post.economics.harvard.edu/faculty/glaeser/papers.html
(accessed April 10, 2005).

attention, and they must be in hand before potential solutions can be effectively addressed or devised.

Drosscape is a companion to *Reclaiming the American West*, which documents the altered-landscape region of the western Unites States as a result of natural-resource extraction.[2] Documenting "mining waste" and speculating about its reuse, *Reclaiming the American West* asserts that by the year 2230 most of the natural resources held in private and public lands in the western U.S. will be mined out for consumption and that the resultant landscape will be designed as a new, reclaimed ecosystem–becoming the largest infrastructural project of the next quarter millennium. *Reclaiming* reveals the enormous new landscapes forming in the wake of an industrial process (mining). It attempts to burn the magnitude of this process into the public's conscience in order to make the case for creative ways to redesign post-mined landscapes. Waste produced through mining (from pits to waste-rock piles, from haul roads to buildings, and from altered ecologies to polluted waterways) can, in many cases, be safely, opportunistically, functionally, and aesthetically reclaimed and redesigned for post-mine occupation and reuse.

It is natural that *Drosscape*, which also explores topics of landscape and waste, should follow the first book. The story of its genesis is serendipitous. Researching material for *Reclaiming the American West* took me into flight for more than five years, conducting fieldwork and aerial photography throughout the U.S. Intermountain West. Although many of these trips routed into remote areas where mining takes place, the municipal and private airports I flew from were typically located on the periphery of large urbanized areas. In order to be prepared for arrival over the mining sites I loaded my film, advanced a few frames, and adjusted the film speed and camera settings for the day's weather and sunlight conditions. After developing the films, I discovered that the first few frames–and often the last few–revealed a variety of interesting, if not disturbing, landscape conditions around the peripheries of the cities from which I flew. At first I did not realize how widespread the situation actually was and then I found several hundred of these images (previously cast aside) in a box next to my light table. The images revealed landscape conditions of monstrous proportions and startling similarities that transcended geographic differences. I knew then that another project loomed. Five years of research and fieldwork later produced the present project, *Drosscape*. All of my research and fieldwork grows from firsthand experience of the contemporary American landscape. These landscapes are too newly created, too large in scale, and too full of adjacencies and complexities to study from library or office settings. All of the photographs in this book were carefully researched and selected to reveal evidence of the landscape conditions discussed herein.

Further inspiration for this book came from my students, who over the years have expressed dismay and bewilderment at the lack of critical discourse on the

[2] Alan Berger, *Reclaiming the American West* (New York: Princeton Architectural Press, 2002).

topic of urbanism and urbanization within the profession of landscape architecture. Around the world, educational venues for landscape architecture lack substantial depth concerning urbanization. As a response to this problem I began offering a course at Harvard Design School geared toward students in the landscape degree programs. Entitled "Landscapes of Urbanization," the course allows students to study urbanism from a landscape architect's perspective.

Drosscape divides roughly into three parts. Part One: Landscape, Urbanization, and Waste is qualitative. Its goal is to link the practical and theoretical issues concerning urbanization and waste landscape, so that the reader can make associations among industrial, economic, and consumption activity and the landscapes created as a result of these processes. It introduces and explains the ways in which contemporary modes of industrial production, driven by economical and consumerist influences, contribute to urbanization and the formation of waste landscapes–meaning actual *waste* (such as municipal solid waste, sewage, scrap metal, etc.), *wasted* places (such as abandoned or contaminated sites), or *wasteful* places (such as huge parking lots or retail malls). The term *urban sprawl* and the rhetoric of pro- and anti-urban sprawl advocates are described by me as obsolete when it comes to dealing with these conditions.

Part Two: Representing the Relationships between Waste Landscape and Urbanization is composed of two chapters. Chapter three offers quantitative and visual analyses of ten major U.S. urbanized regions, spread across diverse geographical areas: north to south, east to west. Waste landscape, as defined in part one, is represented by combining geo-spatial technologies with U.S. Census data, creating a new spatio-economic composite reading of each city's special "waste geography." Chapter four is composed of short essays about waste landscapes accomplished by photographic evidence. This chapter reveals waste landscapes across topical origins (Landscapes of Dwelling, Landscapes of Transition, Landscapes of Infrastructure, Landscapes of Obsolescence, Landscapes of Exchange, and Landscapes of Contamination) that may jibe with readers' personal experience; the goal being to identify waste landscapes for future recycling.

Part Three: The Drosscape Manifesto introduces *drosscape*, a term for a new design paradigm that emphasizes the productive integration and re-use of waste landscapes in the urban world. The methodology behind designing with drosscapes explicitly uses the discoveries made in part two, the regional waste geographies (chapter three) and topical waste landscapes (chapter four), as the loci for future urban landscape design and planning activity. The etymological lineage of the words *vast*, *waste*, and *dross* provide the reader with a greater understanding of the terms' contemporary value in describing the urban world. The stage is thus set for designing with waste landscape as a central activity. Strategies for designing for drosscapes are introduced and described as a bottom-up advocacy process, suggesting a move away from the heroic, modernist, master-planner toward the designer who engenders inventiveness, entrepreneurialism, and long-term environmental recovery.

Acknowledgments

In addition to the people named throughout this book, many of whose ideas are discussed in part one, the following colleagues have encouraged me, challenged my imagination, corrected my errors, and enriched my intellectual journey into the urban world. I give special thanks to Frederick Turner and Albert Pope for their critical insights during manuscript development. Thanks to Dorion Sagan and Gene Bressler for reading the first manuscript. I am indebted to Casey Brown, Rachel Loeffler, and Elizabeth Fain, graduates of the Harvard Design School. Casey unselfishly dedicated the better part of three years assisting me in the overwhelming task of researching and deciphering the complex geospatial data and U.S. Census materials that underpin the graphics in this book. I also thank the colleagues who have generously and enthusiastically shared their ideas over the past few years. They include Lars Lerup, David Luberoff, Michael Jensen, Jerold Kayden, Edward Glaeser, Richard Zeckhauser, Richard Sommer, Margaret Crawford, Marco Cenzatti, Dwayne Nuzum, Alan Altshuler, Niall Kirkwood, Dan Schrag, Charles Waldheim, James Corner, Robert Poole, George Hargreaves, Richard Forman, Carl Steinitz, and John Stilgoe.

I thank the Cessna aircraft pilots who safely flew me across the urbanized landscape of America, skillfully negotiating with air-traffic controllers while permitting me to hang out open windows in order to obtain the photographs in this book. In the post-9/11 security climate, their knowledge of terrain and willingness to fly into difficult navigational situations were crucial to accessing many of the image locations. Sadly, it is becoming more difficult to obtain images of infrastructure and industrial sites, especially in urban areas and from ground perspectives.

The Harvard Design School's Department of Landscape Architecture and junior-faculty grants provided research and production support. Harvard University's Tozier Fund provided funding for film conversion. Funding for aerial photography came from Harvard Design School's dean grants. This book has been generously supported by the A. Alfred Taubman Center for State and Local Government at Harvard's Kennedy School of Government and Harvard University Center for the Environment.

My gratitude goes out to Kevin Lippert, publisher of Princeton Architectural Press, and my editor Jennifer Thompson, who have worked with me on two successive book projects. They have ensured the highest quality production of the complex graphic content that runs throughout my research. I am fortunate to swim twice in the deep, committed talent pool at PAP. And many thanks to Adam Michaels and Prem Krishnamurthy of Project Projects for their inspired book design.

Finally, I thank my wife, Elaine, daughter, Leah, and family, who remain a constant source of energy and inspiration in my life.

All photographs are taken by the author between 2003 and 2005 using a Contax 645 camera with various speeds of Fuji Velvia film.

Part One
Landscape, Urbanization, and Waste

Part One
Landscape, Urbanization, and Waste

Who are those hooded hordes swarming
Over endless plains, stumbling in cracked earth
Ringed by the flat horizon only
What is the city over the mountains
–T. S. Elliot, *The Waste Land*

The Changing Nature of Urban Land

The American landscape is rapidly urbanizing. Over the last fifty years, population density in urbanized areas has dropped by more than 50 percent, while the highest rates of population growth developed at the edges of metropolitan areas. As long ago as 1970, the U.S. Census found that more people live in newly urbanized areas than in central cities or small towns. It is estimated that more than 62 percent of the American population lives in newly urbanized areas, whereas 38 percent live in older center cities. Strikingly similar percentages of people are employed in these respective places.[1] In a recent study of 213 urbanized areas, it was discovered that between 1960 and 1990 the total population increased from 95 million to 140 million (47 percent), while urbanized land increased from 25,000 square miles to 51,000 square miles (107 percent).[2] This means that urbanized density per square mile decreased in the U.S. by 28 percent during that time. These trends continue to accelerate. Between 1982 and 1992, the annual conversion rate of undeveloped land to developed land was 1.4 million acres per year. Between 1992 and 1997, the total land converted to developed land was 11.2 million acres; this equates to a development rate of 2.2 million acres per year (see figure 1).[3]

The flight from center cities to newly urbanized ground is a phenomenon not restricted or limited to America. The Brazilian megacity of São Paulo, for example, is so congested and crime-ridden (8,500 murders per year!) that many affluent families have moved to its undeveloped periphery and purchased helicopters as a means to avoid gridlock and carjackings. São Paulo's four hundred personal helicopters is the fastest-growing fleet in the world.[4] Toronto, San Diego, Denver, Melbourne, and hundreds of other urbanized regions have meanwhile built private highway and roadway systems to link suburban residents with city centers. Some of these toll highways have real-time congestion pricing systems, which adjust the toll rates

[1] 2000 U.S. Census. For a more opinionated analysis see F. Kaid Benfield, Donald D. T. Chen, Matthew D. Raimi, *Once There Were Greenfields: How Urban Sprawl Is Undermining America's Environment, Economy, and Social Fabric* (New York: Natural Resource Defense Council, 1999).
[2] Ralph E. Heimlich and William D. Anderson, *Development at the Urban Fringe and Beyond: Impacts on Agriculture and Rural Land*, Agricultural Economic Report No. AER803 (Washington DC: Resource Economics Division, Economic Research Service, USDA, June, 2001), http://www.ers.usda.gov/publications/aer803/ (accessed April 20, 2004).
[3] Marlow Vesterby and Kenneth S. Krupa, *Major Uses of Land in the United States*, Statistical Bulletin No. 973 (Washington DC: Resource Economics Division, Economic Research Service, USDA, 1997).
[4] Stephen Graham and Simon Marvin, *Splintering Urbanism* (London: Routledge, 2001), 5–6.

to peak and off-peak commuting hours as a means of ensuring less traffic in the lanes charging the highest fare.[5] Once a North American phenomenon, gated suburban communities are now found in Istanbul, Dubai, Manila, Jakarta, Tokyo, Johannesburg, and Mumbai (Bombay), among dozens of other locations.[6]

New cities are forming faster than scholarly theories can be published to explain them. Politicians, environmentalists, geographers, farmers, designers, and many other groups associated with land development struggle with generating a vocabulary to describe the causes and effects of rapid horizontal urbanization.

1—Urban Land Surfaces in the U.S.
Between 1960 and 1990 the total population increased from 95 million to 140 million (47 percent), while urbanized land increased from 25,000 square miles to 51,000 square miles (107 percent).

Central Cities
Urbanized Areas, 1990
Urbanized Areas, 2000

[5] See the following sources for information on privatized highway construction and financing: web site"I-15 FasTrak Online" (web site for Southern California's Interstate 15 and automated toll use), http://fastrak.sandag.org/ (accessed June 14, 2005); Robert W. Poole, Jr. "California Toll Roads Take Opposite Paths," on the web site of Reason Public Policy Institute (RPPI), http://www.rppi.org; Jon Caldara, "Metro Traffic May Get Hot, Hot, Hot: Toll Lanes Could Eliminate Highway Jams," http://www.denverpost.com. (accessed June 15, 2003); The international business guide to public-private partnerships in infrastructure finance, *PWFinancing*, provides updates on privatized roadway concessions, reporting that there have been 203 awarded since 1985, see *Public Works Financing, Major Projects Database*, "Private Toll Roads Worldwide" (Westfield, N.J.: PWF Financing, 2004).
[6] Graham and Marvin, *Splintering Urbanism*, 5–6.

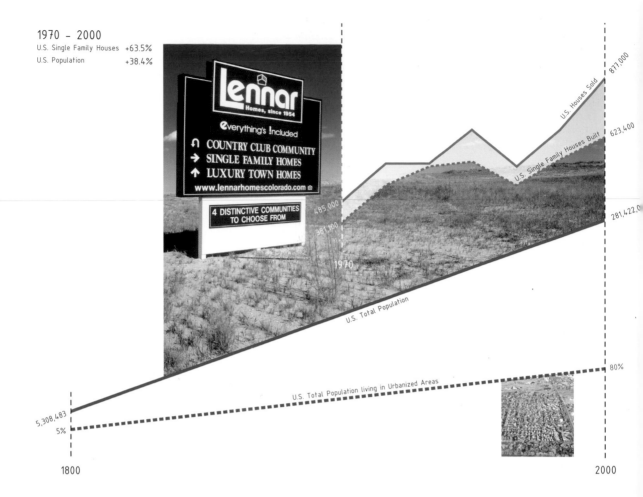

1970 – 2000
U.S. Single Family Houses +63.5%
U.S. Population +38.4%

877,000
U.S. Houses Sold
623,400
U.S. Single Family Houses Built
485,000
381,100
281,422,0
1970
U.S. Total Population
U.S. Total Population living in Urbanized Areas
80%
5,308,483
5%

1800   2000

This vocabulary has, in many cases, further obfuscated and polarized the issue. Hundreds of acronyms and abbreviated names have emerged to describe the organizational structures, processes, and technical aspects of urbanization. The list of acronyms is well over a thousand long when linked to other systems, such as global trading, trucking and shipping, and economic policy and treatises.[7] Some of the more popular acronyms and abbreviated names include **PDR (purchase of development rights), UA (urbanized area), NRC (neighborhood retail center), PUD (planned unit development), CID (common interest development), and MPO (metropolitan planning organization).** There are literally hundreds of terms used for what was once simply referred to as the "city" (see Appendix 1). As Robert Lang notes, "The new metropolis is such a conceptual mess and so difficult to grasp that…in a 1992 conference on the suburbs, over 200 names were listed that identified the entirety or elements of the new metropolis."[8]

2—Landscape Urbanization in the U.S.
Over the past century America's urbanized environments have evolved from dense, vertical, and architecturally dominated places to the horizontal opposite. Single family homes built from 1970 to 2000 grew nearly 64 percent, while population only increased by 38 percent.

[7] For additional acronyms see U.S. Agency for International Development, http://www.usaid.gov/pubs/cbj2002/abbr_acron.html (accessed June 14, 2004). U.S. Department of State, "The Language of Trade," http://usinfo.state.gov/products/pubs/trade/acron.htm (accessed June 14, 2004). Friends of the Earth, "The Citizens' Guide to Trade, Environment and Sustainability," http://www.foei.org/trade/ activistguide/acronyms.htm (accessed June 14, 2004). The American Planning Association, http://www.planning.org/resources-k/acronyms.htm (accessed June 14, 2004).
[8] Robert Lang, "Edgeless Cities: Exploring the Elusive Metropolis," (paper presented at the Taub Urban Research Center, New York: New York University, October 2000).

In consideration of all these names and their descriptions, it is clear that the American city continues to change forms. As a result, perceptions and values about urbanization change as well (see figure 2). America's urbanized environments have over the past century evolved from dense, vertical, and architecturally dominated places to the horizontal opposite. This condition was recently described by the *New York Times* as a new category of city, the "micropolis," is comprised of "locales having a core city of fewer than 50,000 (as small as 10,000)" and is economically and politically important enough to become a new category for U.S. Census data gathering.[9] The main distinguishing factor of today's horizontal city is the increasing amount of surface area, or landscape, that it takes to accommodate fewer people. The majority of these surfaces serve no overt functional purpose. They merely appear as "leftovers" from development.

Scholarship regarding urbanism is shifting toward landscape and away from architecture as many find that rapid horizontal urbanization escapes traditional descriptions of the city as a place of concentrated population, bundled infrastructure, architectural density, and centralized government.[10] Put simply, cities don't look or function the same anymore. A key concept of this metamorphosis is termed *urban sprawl.* The types of development found in sprawling areas mainly consist of horizontally oriented landscape planes and surfaces, rather than vertically dense buildings (see figure 3).

Sprawl is predominantly a horizontal landscape phenomenon. This thesis deserves further articulation because people concerned with landscape, environment, and sustainability issues almost never consider sprawl a positive opportunity, even though it is largely dominated by landscape development.

The Obsolescence of Sprawl

The term sprawl is typically used when describing the negative effects of unplanned, uncontrolled, or market-driven development. Is sprawl inherently bad? And if so, in what ways? What are the good attributes, if any, of sprawl? Many definitions assume sprawl is a suburban phenomenon essentially detached from its urban core, the city proper. I will argue that this is simply not true anymore. Urbanization is urbanization, whether in the form of low-rise suburban-planned unit developments or high-rise central-business-district apartment buildings.

A number of scholars insist that the term suburbia inaccurately describes urbanization outside cities.

[9] Jon Gertner, "The Micropolis," *New York Times Magazine*, December 12, 2004.
[10] Refer to the new body of publications (since roughly 2001) on the subject of landscape urbanism. Other examples include a conference titled *World Urbanization & Landscape Architecture: A Symposium on Contemporary Urbanization & Future Practices of Landscape Architecture*, co-sponsored in 2002 by the University of Pennsylvania's Department of Landscape Architecture and Regional Planning. (Although only two–out of twelve–landscape scholars presented at this conference, the audience consisted of landscape architecture professionals and students.) The University of Toronto, in 2003, advertised a full-time teaching position for a landscape urbanist. London's heralded Architectural Association has a new landscape urbanism program. Architecture is now awash with landscape discourse, from sustainability issues and green architecture to "field" organization and network theory.

As writer Joel Garreau argues, suburban sprawl is not "sub" to anything anymore.[11] In fact, if one evaluates categories of urban[ization] growth through empirical, visual, or experiential means it is the traditional city center that may now be considered subordinate to the urban sprawl that it had originally defined. For better and worse, today's suburban environments often provide more services, diverse amenities, and newer infrastructure. As a result, job markets have increasingly moved from traditional downtowns to outlying suburban areas.[12]

Sprawl is commonly misperceived as merely a housing phenomenon. Outlying office space has been referred to as its own "commercial geography" (see figure 4). In the U.S., seventeen non-downtown areas have more than ten million square feet of office space and another forty-one outlying areas have from five to ten million square feet of office space.[13] Sprawl is also misperceived as caused by banking policy and mortgage subsidies. It has been attributed to federal highway policy, or what has been termed *highway federalism*.[14] That is, federal policies have historically been blamed for the funding of roadways and highways outside densely populated urban centers for defense and other purposes. But this explains neither the growing number of highways built without federal funding nor the reduction of the federal excise tax on gasoline, used to pay for highway construction.[15] Rather, sprawl is better linked with drastically reduced transportation costs and the relocation of manufacturing and industry away from city centers and toward outlying areas (discussed further in chapter 3).[16]

Sprawl affects all of the major development and land-use markets: housing, office, infrastructure, manufacturing, and industry. In Western capitalist culture, sprawl is positioned as the omnipresent and primary phenomenon that contributes to the demise of the older, traditional forms of the central, core city. Encouraged by their lobbying successes, anti-urbanization advocates positioned themselves around negative conceptions of the term sprawl, which has

[11] Joel Garreau, *Edge City* (New York: Doubleday, 1991).
[12] Robert E. Lang, *Edgeless Cities* (Washington, DC: Brookings Institution Press, 2003), 88–100. See also Lang, "Office Sprawl: The Evolving Geography of Business," *Center on Urban & Metropolitan Policy, Brookings Institute Survey Series* (Washington, DC: Brookings Institution Press, 2000); and "Beyond Edge City: Office Sprawl in South Florida," *Center on Urban & Metropolitan Policy, Brookings Institute Survey Series* (Washington, DC: Brookings Institution Press, 2003).
[13] Lang, *Edgeless Cities*, 89–92.
[14] Owen D. Gutfreund, *Twentieth-Century Sprawl: Highways and the Reshaping of the American Landscape* (New York: Oxford University Press, 2004), 1-30. Also see Alex Marshall, *How Cities Work* (Austin: University of Texas Press, 2000). One of the earliest examples of this perception can be read in Lewis Mumford, "The Highway and the City," *Architectural Record*, April 1958, 179–82. Other reasons linking federal highway funding to peripheral development are associated with national defense measures, such as "The Only Real Defense," *Bulletin of Atomic Scientists* (1951), 242–87. Also see Ludwig Hilberseimer "Cities and Defense" (c. 1945) in *The Shadow of Mies: Ludwig Hilberseimer, Architect, Educator and Urban Planner*, ed. Richard Pommer, David Spaeth, and Kevin Harrington (New York/ Chicago: Rizolli/Art Institute of Chicago, 1988), 89–93.
[15] Based on inflation, the federal gasoline excise tax has been decreasing over its life span, thus allowing less federal funding for highway construction. In the U.S., the federal gasoline tax is 18.4 cents a gallon, and the gasoline taxes in the various states range from 10 cents to 30 cents, averaging about 22 cents a gallon.
[16] Glaeser and Kohlhase, "Cities, Regions and the Decline of Transport Costs."

been accepted far more effectively than any other descriptive term. Across disciplines and audiences, sprawl is seen as an inherently negative phenomenon, associated with rapid horizontal urbanization.

Why?

In my quest to determine why sprawl is widely considered a negative phenomenon, I combed through the contemporary literature most often cited by anti-sprawl advocates. My question is answered in as many different ways as there are people writing anti-sprawl rhetoric. Compounding this is the recent proliferation of pro-sprawl literature. For instance, on the hotly contested topic of agricultural land consumption one finds strong empirical cases built by sprawl stakeholders. According to the American Farmland Trust, an organization that represents farming interests, the U.S. continues each year to lose nearly one million acres of farmland and open space to urban expansion.[17] The Department of Agriculture uses the same statistic to argue that although one million acres of land are lost to development each year since 1960, urban expansion has not been seen as a threat to most farming because the loss of land may only reduce production of a few specialty crops.[18] Moreover, the Environmental

3—Los Angeles, California
Urban sprawl is predominantly a landscape phenomenon. The types of development found in "sprawling areas" mainly consist of horizontally oriented landscape planes and surfaces, not buildings (notably vertical density).

[17] See the "Stop Sprawl" report by the Sierra Club (fall 2000) http://www.sierraclub.org/sprawl/50statesurvey/intro.asp (accessed August 15, 2001).
[18] Heimlich and Anderson, Development at the Urban Fringe and Beyond: Impacts on Agriculture and Rural Land, http://www.ers.usda.gov/publications/aer803/.

Protection Agency (EPA) blames current farming practices for 70 percent of the pollution in the nation's rivers and streams. The agency reports that farmland runoff of chemicals, silt, and animal waste has polluted more than 173,000 miles of waterways.[19] The Sierra Club, America's oldest, largest, and most influential grassroots environmental organization, has the country's most comprehensive web site addressing "smart growth" and "stop sprawl" advocacy issues and strongly supports the preservation of farmland.[20] Of course, over longer periods of time, farmland is itself artificial, the representation of a human agricultural technology developed some 10,000 years ago, which led directly to the earliest cities and replaced biodiverse communities with those of food crops. On the one hand, the essence of conservatism is an attempt to preserve the past in which our ancestors flourished; on the other hand, life from its inception has been marked by growth and change. In a sense, sprawl is the unintended consequence, the overflow or spillover of urbanization. But such overflows, in a larger, evolutionary context, are the inevitable result of life's expansionist, waste-making tendencies.

The anti-sprawl and pro-sprawl rhetoric and its adherents are sharply polarized. Little room is left

4—Fulton/Dekalb County line, Georgia
The Georgia 400 Corridor is a commercial corridor mostly composed of non-downtown office space, light industrial businesses, and manufacturing establishments. Downtown Atlanta is in the background.

[19] Leo Horrigan, Robert S. Lawrence, and Polly Walker, "How Sustainable Agriculture Can Address the Environmental and Human Health Harms of Industrial Agriculture," *Environmental Health Perspectives*, 110, no. 5 (Baltimore: Johns Hopkins University's Center for a Livable Future Publications, May 2002).
[20] See the official web site for the Sierra Club, http://www.sierraclub.com.

for debate or speculation from distinct, nonpartisan perspectives. Indeed, the rhetoric has become so politically charged that it has rendered the term sprawl all but meaningless. My goal is not to dwell on polarized sprawl rhetoric, which is not productive in advancing knowledge on urbanization. The language and subsequent polemics of sprawl veil opportunities for finding the overlapping values and interests, of pro- and anti-sprawl constituencies. Regardless of one's position or use of the term, sprawl is a real phenomenon that deserves more substantial consideration.

The following paragraphs stretch entrenched notions of urbanism, city, suburb, and sprawl toward a new vocabulary for the horizontal city. They begin the process of salvaging an in-between landscape. One needs to understand that any new naming system runs the risk of fetishizing itself, just as mainstream discourses on the city, particularly on sprawl, have inspired an irrational reification. This is not my intention. My purpose is rather to provide readers with a cursory understanding of the terminology that is emerging around landscapes associated with the horizontal city and to disseminate into the public realm select ideas that would otherwise remain squelched by pro- and anti-sprawl zealots or become buried in journals read by narrow audiences. The new terms are meant to initiate a conversation about landscape and urbanization, from which anyone may make more informed real-world decisions to affect design.

This text will not follow any particular order related to development type (i.e., housing first, office second, and so forth) that might imply some kind of linear sequence or cause-and-effect pattern. As previously stated, the horizontal city consists of any number and mixture of these land uses; they are all interrelated in some capacity. One need not single out a concept or development type as the problem or solution to urbanization, but he or she may regard all the concepts as a working language to be improved, refined, and extended by others. Some ideas will be relatively obvious and translatable into practice and physical form. Others will have to remain for now in the realm of theory, somewhere between the material and immaterial. Regardless, the collective body of terms, ideas, and theories put forth in this book, represents a new discourse for better understanding the relationships of landscape and urbanization.

Chapter One
Discourses for Landscape and Urbanization

What is *place* in this new "in-between" world?
–Nigel Thrift, *Writing The Rural*

Home was BAMA, the Sprawl, the Boston-Atlanta Metropolitan Axis.
–William Gibson, *Neuromancer*

The Horizontal City and the In-Between

At the beginning of the twenty-first century, as well as
in Gibson's prognosticated future, the American city
is characterized by rapid horizontal growth, having a
dispersed and sparsely populated surface of activities.[1]
The resultant landscape is difficult to describe in
words. Everyone who dwelled in or traveled through
and around urbanized areas in America, however, is
familiar with this landscape. It may be vacant strips
alongside roadways, seas of parking lots, unused land,
surfaces awaiting development, dumping grounds,
warehouse districts, a seemingly endless stretch of
setbacks and perimeters framing housing communities.
Seen at the *local* scale, (e.g. walking or driving through
one's neighborhood or shopping district) the landscape
of the horizontal city may appear diminished and
wasteful. It appears poorly planned, designed, and
unmaintained and as irregular and indiscreet leftovers
from other, more dominant forms of development like
buildings or highways. Viewed at the metropolitan,
or *regional*, scale, (e.g. from the top of a tall building
or airplane) the landscape of the horizontal city often
appears as extensive and plentiful–open space and
vegetation–such as large agricultural tracts surrounded
by new development or forests with office parks nestled
in their interior.

The "building out" of the horizontal city has formed
a new frontier across the American landscape. This
frontier embodies characteristics both internal (within
the built-out zone) and external (beyond the leading
edge of development) to the horizontal city. The *internal*
frontier emerges from the composite of many landscape
fragments within the local urbanized area: strips, lots,
and unbuilt or unbuildable properties (see figure 5). With
the exception of large public parks and protected open
space, the unbuilt portions of the urbanized landscape
have become smaller in aggregate size, increasingly
marginalized *in-between* architectural objects in the
urban fabric.[2] This reduction may be attributed to many

[1] One of the earliest examples of this characterization was published in
1958 by the editors of *Fortune* magazine. Originally appearing as a series
of articles in 1957, *The Exploding Metropolis* is one of the early post–World
War II volumes to document urban growth as chaotic, disorderly, unnatural,
and problematic. See *The Exploding Metropolis* (New York: Doubleday,
1958). See especially William H. Whyte's essay "Urban Sprawl," 133–56.
[2] This does not mean that urbanization is good or bad, but that it could be
a more sustainable endeavor if landscape were incorporated in a more
substantial way. See Chris Berdik, "Give me Land, Lots of Land…" *Boston
Globe*, June 12, 2005, H1, 4. And Richard T. T. Forman, *Land Mosaics:
The Ecology of Landscapes and Regions* (Cambridge: Cambridge
University Press, 1995). This book views landscapes leftover from urban
development practices as having potential ecological benefits. I argue
that his type of landscape sustainability is a form of reclamation, since it
appears after development and market capitalism run their course.

factors, such as the planning and zoning codes that restrict the ways landscape can be incorporated into development. It may also be the result of the new transportation or manufacturing trends (such as agglomerations), or land's economic value.[3] In general, urban land with income-generating structures is worth more to taxing authorities and private developers than vacant lands. At the same time, public or private entities speculate and may leave land strategically vacant until market conditions warrant sale or development. The outcome then is another kind of aggregated patchwork.

The *external* frontier of the American landscape was once collectively considered the vast continental stretch of open land outside the largest centralized cities–the city's Other. This frontier evolved into what we experience today as a fragmented entity, best described as the landscape existing between nodes of urbanization. Today's external frontier exhibits a closer proximity of each urbanized area to its neighboring one, or what geographers Stephen Graham and Simon Marvin describe as the more totally urbanized world.[4] The external frontier is neither here nor there

5—Downtown Fort Worth, Texas
The internal frontier emerges from the composite of many landscape fragments within the local urbanized area—strips, lots, and territories leftover from past and present politico-economical regimes.

[3] For an understanding of manufacturing trends see: Sukkoo Kim, "Expansion of Markets and the Geographic Distribution of Economic Activities: The Trends in U.S. Regional Manufacturing Structure, 1860–1987," *The Quarterly Journal of Economics*, 110, no. 4, (Cambridge: MIT Press, 1995), 881-908; Glaeser and Kohlhase, "Cities, Regions and the Decline of Transport Costs," 2003.
[4] Graham and Marvin, *Telecommunications and the City* (New York: Routledge, 1996), 378.

(see figure 6). Some three decades ago, realizing that urban growth and land use changes are much more than visual problems, geographer Pierce Lewis identified the disappearance of clear boundaries between city and country. Lewis writes, "The boundary that has separated city from country throughout American history is now almost gone, and that is true whether one talks about physical boundaries or about more subtle forms of intellectual or psychological boundaries. To some degree, in most parts of America's inhabited domain the metropolis is almost everywhere."[5] Lewis's contention is that today's city is so diffuse that it has become a "galactic metropolis," a city-form resembling a galaxy of stars and planets, with large empty areas in-between, held together with something akin to gravitational attraction.[6] These "large empty areas" are what he terms new metropolitan tissue, or areas that do not lay directly adjacent to existing nucleated cities but often lie great distances from city centers. Lewis asks the reader to accept the fact that this tissue is here to stay as the result of the horizontal urbanization, and he provokes readers to rethink its use. Lewis's "tissue," of course, hauntingly fits the description of the external frontier.

Internal and external frontiers should not all be salvaged by society. Landscape attributes of these frontiers are indistinct: they are regarded either as too small and fragmented at the local scale or aggregated into isolation at the regional scale. It is difficult for society to identify and value them. The traditional way to value urban landscapes is by using landscape as a placemaking medium (such as a small-scale public park or plaza). Today, this idea is blurred. The landscape of the contemporary horizontal city is no longer a placemaking or condensing medium. Instead it is fragmented and chaotically spread throughout the city in small bits and pieces. Because it is so difficult to see in its entirety, the contemporary city's landscape escapes wholeness and public consciousness, once poignantly referred to as "terra incognita."[7]

But since it plays a necessary role in urban evolution, why is the in-between undervalued. Because it is the exact opposite of a vertical sight for sore eyes (such as a deteriorating building), the in-between landscape lies flat around such objects and is thus likely to dissuade close inspection. Publicity campaigns for cities always depict institutional buildings, cultural centers, airports, even sports stadia as the most valuable cultural attractions. A city's landscape assets–public parks, golf courses, water bodies, tree-lined promenades, pedestrian malls, and conservation greenways–typically serve as the stage supporting these attractions. Missing are the unsightly but crucial transitional landscapes such as railroad yards, vacant lots, derelict buildings, contaminated fields, smokestacks, industrial manufacturing and parking lots. Or, as stated above, these transitional landscapes are simply ignored.

6—Housing along Loop 202 and the south side of Phoenix South Mountain Park, Chandler / Phoenix, Arizona
The external frontier begins on the periphery of urbanization. The undeveloped area to the left is the property of the Gila River Indian Reservation.

[5] Pierce Lewis, "The Galactic Metropolis," *Beyond the Urban Fringe: Land Use Issues of Nonmetropolitan America*, ed. Rutherford Platt and George Macinko, 23 (Minneapolis: University of Minnesota Press, 1983).
[6] Ibid., 34.
[7] Ann O'M. Bowman and Michael A. Pagano, *Terra Incognita: Vacant Land and Urban Strategies* (Washington, DC: Georgetown University Press, 2004).

A Liminal Landscape

Liminality is frequently likened to death, to being in the womb,
to invisibility, to darkness, to bisexuality, to the wilderness, and
to an eclipse of the sun or moon.
–Victor W. Turner, *The Ritual Process*

Much of the landscape surface left in the wake of rapid
horizontal urbanization is not a clearly defined, stable,
and fixed entity. It is between occupancies and uses,
successional phases, and (dis)investment cycles. The term
in-between describes a state of liminality, something that
lives in transition and eludes classification, something
that resists new stability and reincorporation. The
in-between landscapes of the horizontal city are liminal
because they remain at the margins (or *limen*, which
means "threshold" in Latin), awaiting a societal desire to
inscribe them with value and status.[8]

A deeper conception of the liminal landscape is
achieved by understanding a cultural analogy described in
the work of anthropologist Victor W. Turner. He explains
that the liminal condition relates to the formation of
communitas, the Latin term for community.[9] In his seminal
book *The Ritual Process*, Turner reveals that all transitions,
or rites of passage, in tribal cultures are marked by three
phases: separation, liminality, and aggregation.

> The first phase (of separation) comprises symbolic
> behavior signifying the detachment of the individual
> or group either from an earlier fixed point in the
> social structure, from a set of cultural conditions
> (a "state"), or from both. During the intervening
> "liminal" period, the characteristics of the ritual
> subject (the "passenger") are ambiguous; he passes
> through a cultural realm that has few or none of
> the attributes of the past or coming state. In the
> third phase (reaggregation or reincorporation),
> the passage is consummated. The ritual subject,
> individual or corporate, is in a relatively stable
> state once more and, by virtue of this, has rights
> and obligations vis-à-vis others of a clearly defined
> and "structural" type; he is expected to behave
> in accordance with certain customary norms and
> ethical standards binding on incumbents of social
> positions in a system of such positions.[10]

Turner suggests that tribes perform rituals as a means
of inscribing knowledge and wisdom in their people.
This goal is often achieved by destroying the previous
status of an individual in order to prepare him or her for
their new responsibilities and tribal privileges. According
to Turner, the liminal period of the ritual is the most
critical. The ritual subjects, or passenger[s], are "shown
that in themselves they are clay or dust, mere matter,
whose form is impressed upon them by society."[11] It is
in this phase that everyday life and normal activity are
confronted through "socially subversive and ritually
inverse acts."[12] The passenger is then reincorporated into
tribal hierarchy. In Turner's synthesis, the liminal phase

[8] Victor W. Turner, *The Ritual Process* (New York: Aldine De Gruyter, 1969), 94.
[9] Ibid., 96.
[10] Ibid., 94.
[11] Ibid., 103.
[12] Roger D. Abrahams, Foreword, *The Ritual Process*, ix.

of the ritual is performed in-between the "detachment" and "reaggregation" phases.

There are many activities in contemporary society that fit Turner's rubric of liminal-phase "subversive and inversive acts." Not surprisingly, these acts all originate and flourish within the margins of an otherwise ordinary and homogeneous urban environment. One example is the "smart mob."[13] Smart mobs are amorphous, decentralized networks of people and groups who connect to one another and coordinate in a collective action, such as a political protest.[14] They are groups of people carrying wireless communication devices. They swarm and act in concert on vast scales. Using text messaging and the Internet, smart mobs have no centralized authority or leader and no headquarters or "place" in which to meet. They connect at locations determined by the collective action. A second example of a smart mob is the cycling event Critical Mass. Hundreds, sometimes thousands, of bikers take to city streets on a monthly basis to promote nonpolluting transportation. Critical Mass participants admit that the rides have no planned routes, that they have no formal organization or leaders, and that the streets are their meeting locale.[15] A third example is word-of-mouth research, advertising, and marketing strategies, practiced by organizations such as New York–based BuzzMetrics. The general idea behind word-of-mouth advertising is the promotion of brand recognition through grassroots adoption and word of mouth, not through traditional advertising venues. The Boston-based word-of-mouth firm, BzzAgent, developed a proprietary software called BzzEngine that accumulates data from specific trendsetting people as they travel the Internet, leaving messages on bulletin-board pages, altering personal web sites, and exchanging e-mail lists.[16] This information assists companies and their advertising strategists in rapidly identifying and responding to emerging markets. Word-of-mouth marketing also takes place in physical locations, such as households and informal gatherings, that strategically target very specific demographic groups. A recent case study involving a handheld electronic game enlisted three thousand volunteers to share their opinions with family and friends over twelve weeks.[17] Conversely, word-of-mouth campaigns can also be used to detract from a company's products, enabling consumers to vent their frustrations and rally momentum against a particular brand.[18]

The homogenizing effects of the horizontal city (cookie-cutter planning and zoning codes, standardized engineering practices, master planning, etc.) and new communication technologies have led to novel forms of social activities because people do not want to

[13] John Schwartz, "New Economy: In the Tech Meccas, Masses of People, or 'Smart Mobs,' Are Keeping in Touch Through Wireless Devices," New York Times, July 22, 2002.

[14] Jennifer Lee, "The Nation: Critical Mass: How Protesters Mobilized So Many and So Nimbly," New York Times, February 23, 2003.

[15] Colin Moynihan, "Judge Refuses to Halt Mass Ride and Forbids Police to Seize Bicycles," New York Times, October 29, 2004.

[16] BzzAgent's official web site, http://www.bzzagent.com.

[17] Press Release Newswire, a free online press release distribution service for small to medium businesses, http://www.prweb.com/about.php (accessed March 2, 2005).

[18] Nat Ives, "The Media Business: Advertising; Marketing's Flip Side Is the 'Determined Detractor,'" New York Times, December 27, 2004.

spend twenty-four hours a day in the same type of
designed environment. It is easy to understand how
these activities take advantage of a city's landscape
leftovers because urban open space is increasingly
being privatized. In the urbanized world, the in-between
landscape should be valued because it provides a
threshold, or platform, for liminal cultural phenomena
to play out. Thus communitas is cultivated.

7—Gated housing in Houston, Texas
The enclave creates a conceptual and physical
"in-between" through its enforcement of
exclusion. In order for the enclave to function
it must build an infrastructure of separation,
disconnecting itself from its surroundings.

Enclaves, Off Worlds, Ladders
Agriculture, for eight thousand years the primary locus of human and
animal labor, is now secondary to the immense, literally geological
drama of urbanization.
–Mike Davis, *Dead Cities*

There are three terms naturalized by designers
to describe the isolating effects of suburban housing
developments from their surrounding urbanized
areas: enclaves, off worlds, and ladders.

The first term, enclave, is defined as a distinct
territorial, cultural, or social unit enclosed within or
as if within foreign territory, such as a part of a
country lying wholly within the boundaries of another
or a detached mass contained within another
kind of surrounding.[19] Enclave is derived from the
Latin *inclavare*, meaning "to shut in or lock up."[20]

[19] *The Merriam-Webster Dictionary*, New Rev. ed. (Springfield: Merriam-
Webster, Incorporated, 2004).
[20] *American Heritage Dictionary of the English Language*, 4th ed. (New
York: Houghton Mifflin Company, 2000).

Dolores Hayden, professor of American studies at Yale University, has traced the formation of enclaves in architecture and landscape architecture to the communitarian settlements of the 1840s, which sought political and religious secularity. During this period, enclaves were designed as picturesque parks and villas and restricted economic and social diversity.[21] Today the term is most commonly used to describe gated communities, also called suburban fortresses, that prohibit entrance to those having insufficient identification as a resident, visitor, or employee (see figure 7).[22] The enclave creates a conceptual and physical in-between with its enforcement of exclusion. In order for the enclave to function, it must build an infrastructure of separation, disconnecting itself from its surroundings (except for the highly regulated entrance gate).

Mike Davis, an urban theorist and well-known author of several books on Southern California and its environs, borrows the term off worlds from the 1982 movie *Bladerunner* to categorize and describe the lack of social integration built into the regime of the many booming suburbs that have been designed and enforced as enclaves.[23] The quintessential example, cited by Davis and others, is the monstrous Summerlin, a 22,500-acre master-planned community in Las Vegas, Nevada.[24] It has been under development since 1990. As of December 2003, Summerlin had a population of nearly 85,000 people, and it is expected to grow to approximately 160,000 by the projected build-out year 2020. Summerlin has thirty different villages, each with varying amenities (depending on buy-in price), its own library, performing arts center, and endowed cultural center and ballet company. It also has a comprehensive system of perimeter security walls, closed-circuit cameras, and twenty-four-hour manned guard stations at every community entrance. When a breach of security is detected, the outsider to this "off world" is quickly identified and extracted from the property.[25] As in most planned unit developments, strict covenant agreements control the landscape's appearance and regulate functions in public and private areas. In order to preserve a sense of order, control, and taste among its residents, the landscape inside the enclave is maintained *not* to be used–appearing as if it were planned to remain empty (see figures 8, 9).

Albert Pope, urban theorist and professor of architecture at Rice University, takes a radically different view of gated communities.[26] Rather than looking inside the gates to identify a problem, he is interested in what occurs outside the walls of these places. Pope follows the evolution of the gridiron from the nineteenth-century

8—Housing development near Highways 20/85, Buford, Georgia
As with most planned unit developments (PUDs), strict covenant agreements control the landscape's appearance and regulate functions in public and private areas. In order to preserve a sense of order, control, and the taste of its citizens, the landscape inside the enclave is maintained but not meant to be used—a planned emptiness.

9—Housing near Sugarland / Missouri City, Texas
The lake is designed as an internal landscape void.

[21] Dolores Hayden, *Building Suburbia* (New York: Pantheon Books, 2003), 45–70.
[22] Setha Low, *Behind the Gates: Life, Security, and the Pursuit of Happiness in Fortress America* (London: Taylor & Francis, 2003).
[23] Mike Davis, *Dead Cities* (New York: The New Press, 2002), 96–97.
[24] Sam Hall Kaplan, "Summerlin," *Urban Land* 35, no. 9 (September 1994), 14–18. For up-to-date information, http://www.summerlin.com/home.html (accessed June 14, 2005).
[25] Frank Geary, "Summerlin Shooting: Police Shoot Prowler in Gated Community; Man Spotted on Country Club Hills Surveillance Camera," *Las Vegas Review-Journal*, December 6, 2003.
[26] Albert Pope, *Ladders* (New York: Princeton Architectural Press, 1996), especially 178–83.

city outward into the suburban enclaves being built today. The gridiron's transformation, what Pope calls "ladders," occurs where suburban enclaves cut off the continuous expansion of roadway and end development. The result of ladders is the proliferation of voids outside the enclave's walled perimeter, that seem to have little purpose other than separating walled enclaves from one another or acting as "open-space amenities." In both cases, the purpose of the void is to artificially inflate the market value of the land of the inner enclave by claiming the distinction of separation, privacy, and security (see figures 10, 11).

What is significant about Pope's research is that he argues *against* filling in these voids to re-create or extend the gridiron or to form a new aggregated, contiguous city. He promotes further speculation about why these voids are being created and what we can learn from them. If one is to believe that the discontiguous city must be understood before it is completely filled in, then one needs to find ways to better understand and represent the voids, vacancies, inefficiencies, and fragments of landscape left over from development.

Pope isn't the only scholar calling for voids to remain "unfilled" within the horizontal city. Kenneth Frampton, architectural historian and professor of architecture at Columbia University, is concerned by the "flattening out" of cultures and places caused by low-density urbanization. In order to remediate this condition he proposes using landscape reserves as holding grounds, or voids, which are not to be in-filled by development until, if one may read into the Frampton argument, society comes to its senses and acknowledges the destruction it has caused with wasteful development practices.[27]

Urbanization promotes the production of an in-between landscape, which gathers in the planned voids outside housing enclaves and wherever social codes and land-use covenants restrict landscape diversity. Whether we regard these in-between spaces as enclaves, off worlds, ladders, voids, or tissues, their production is clearly imminent.

10—Housing along the south side of Phoenix South Mountain Park, Chandler / Phoenix, Arizona
The mountain park is treated as the external frontier.

11—Housing in Duluth, Georgia / Gwinnett County
Another purpose of a landscape void is to artificially inflate the market value of the land inside the enclave by claiming distinction through separation, privacy, or security.

Terrain Vague, Exaptation, Vacant, Abandoned
There are no inherently religious objects, thoughts, or events; in contemporary culture so much of our world has been "contaminated" with the *mundane* we hardly recognize the quality of the sacred.
–Lynda Sexson, *Ordinarily Sacred*

During the past decade, designers, artists, photographers, and policy makers have become interested in the in-between. In the design world, the late Spanish architect and critic Ignasi de Solà-Morales positioned terrain vague, a French expression from 1970s filmmaking, as his working theory for designing with urban land that appears to be "empty, abandoned space."[28] Solà-Morales saw great potential for understanding the terrains vagues of the metropolis as an architectural opportunity when few others did.

[27] Kenneth Frampton, "Toward an Urban Landscape," *Columbia Documents of Architecture and Theory*, vol. 4 (New York: Columbia University, 1995), 83–93.
[28] Ignasi de Solà-Morales Rubió, "Terrain Vague," *Anyplace*, ed. Cynthia C. Davidson (Cambridge: MIT Press, 1995), 119.

In practice, however, adapting the term for architects and other designers engaged in making urban form, he explains, is problematic. According to Solà-Morales, architects always design to remove this type condition or to solve a place's problems through design. He suggests that architects should instead fight to keep their differences and design to resist planned continuity, using the differences of terrain vague as motivation for the architectural project. Terrain vague recalls the process evolutionary biologists call exaptation, in which a trait or capability, repeated within the context of successful growth and adaptation, becomes co-opted for unforeseen uses. In the animal world, for example, feathers, which occurred first in flightless reptiles within the context of bodily insulation, later became integral to flight. The architectural world's comparative co-opted structure is the spandrel. A spandrel, according to Stephen Jay Gould, is a space arising "as a side-consequence of a prior decision, and not as an explicitly designed feature in itself."[29] Architects use the term to describe left over spaces from the intersection of rounded arches, which hold up domes. These spandrels were exapted as mosaic areas, having nothing to do with their original structural purpose. Such innovation and redirection was the result of previous conditions of excess and material "waste."[30]

12—Industrial land near Lake Calumet, Illinois, about fifteen miles south of downtown Chicago
Terrain vague, a theory of empty and abandoned space, describes urban locales associated with a past economic or industrial status, falling in-between cycles of investment. Specific sites typically include industrial wastelands, vacant and derelict properties, and declining suburban developments.

[29] Stephen Jay Gould, *The Structure of Evolutionary Theory* (Cambridge: Belknap Press, 2002), 1250.
[30] Ibid. Stephen Jay Gould and Richard C. Lewontin, "The Spandrels of San Marco and the Panglossian Paradigm: A Critique of the Adaptationist Programme," *Proceedings of the Royal Society of London*, B 205 (1979), 581–98.

Terrain vague locales are, in a variety of ways, in between. Many are urbanized areas associated with a past economic or industrial status, falling in between cycles of investment. Specific sites typically include industrial wastelands, vacant and derelict properties, and declining suburban developments (see figure 12). Solà-Morales explains that these sites, because they are no longer centers of activity for the city, are largely ignored in mainstream discourses on design. Taken as a wider phenomenon, a city's collective body of older, declining industrialized sites (or sites overlooked by new modes of economic and industrial production) presents an opportunity for designers. Solà-Morales asserts:

> Here only a few residual values survive, despite the total disaffection from the activity of the city. These strange places exist outside the city's effective circuits and productive structures. From the economic point of view, industrial areas, railway stations, ports, unsafe residential neighborhoods, and contaminated places are where the city is no longer.... In short, they are foreign to the urban system, mentally exterior in the physical interior of the city, its negative image, as much a critique as a possible alternative.[31]

Unfortunately, Solà-Morales's theory of terrain vague has gained relatively little interest in architecture and planning circles, especially related to American urbanism. Why? Was his concept too broad or too difficult to translate into architectural practice? Don't architects and planners gain specific knowledge about these types of sites in their training? Or is it that architects and planners simply aren't interested in terrains vagues?

The answers to these questions arguably point to terrain vague having a much clearer translation in landscape discourse (although dissemination of Solà-Morales's theory was not widespread in landscape architecture either). Over the past decade, the confluence of environmental issues and rapid horizontal urbanization has precipitated an interest in terrain vague originating from the discipline of landscape architecture, which has experienced a renaissance in dealing with such sites.[32] Recent conferences at major universities with landscape-architecture degree programs have focused on the reuse and reclamation of many classifications

[31] Solà-Morales Rubió, "Terrain Vague," 120.
[32] Contemporary reading on this topic often involves landscape architects. For design, see Julia Czerniak, ed., *Case: Downsview Park Toronto* (Cambridge: Harvard Graduate School of Design, 2001), 49–89. Alan Berger, March 2001. "Learning from Downsview," *Landscape Architecture* (March 2001), 132, 131. Fresh Kills Design Competition web site http://www.nyc.gov/html/dcp/html/fkl/ada/competition/2_0.html (accessed June 14, 2005). Regarding industrial landscape reclamation: Berger, *Reclaiming the American West*; A. D. Bradshaw, "The Biology of Land Reclamation in Urban Areas," *European Ecological Symposium* (London: Blackwell, 1982), 293–303; and R. P. Gemmell, "The Origin and Botanical Importance of Industrial Habitats," *European Ecological Symposium*, 33–39. John Jakle and David Wilson, "Deindustrialization," *Derelict Landscapes: The Wasting of America's Built Environment*, (Savage, Maryland: Rowman & Littlefield Publishers, 1992), 57–93; Nancy Leigh and Sarah Coffin, "How Many Brownfields are There? Building an Industrial Database," *Journal of Urban Technology* 7, no. 3 (2000), 1–18; Niall Kirkwood, ed. *Manufactured Sites: Rethinking the Post-Industrial Landscape* (London: Spon Press, 2001).

of terrain vague, including landfills, former industrial-manufacturing sites, infrastructural corridors, abandoned and vacant urban land, abandoned and mined landscapes, toxic landscapes, and federal Superfund sites. These activities suggest that contemporary American society may be changing the ways in which it *values* terrain vague and many other types of waste landscapes.

The first step in delineating and reclaiming the potential of these physically excluded sites is to mentally recognize that such waste deposits are an inevitable result of growth. Waste landscape is an indicator of healthy urban growth.[33]

No longer are polluted and toxic landscapes beyond recovery and reinhabitation, as many are now considered valuable city assets. Sites once dismissed as permanently destroyed such as landfills, factories, and industrial-manufacturing sites are in various stages of reclamation for new uses and revenue generation, including housing, retail, and office developments. Vacant strips of land adjacent to transportation or utility infrastructure, such as in a drainage ditch or right-of-way, are reprogrammed for additional activities, such as linear parks, recreation facilities, parking, or advertising. Inner-city vacant lots and derelict buildings are adaptively reused and converted to productive new forms. The city of Cleveland, for example, created a land bank program to sustain its urban revitalization goals (see figure 13). This program allows the city to repossess vacant land and derelict buildings that are foreclosed and tax delinquent. The city then sells these parcels to its citizens (for redevelopment) from $1 to $100 depending on the lot type.[34]

Studying the amount and significance of vacant urban land (from abandonment or dereliction) in the U.S. was of little interest until the late 1990s. Until this time, there was no significant scholarship on the subject. In 1999, Lincoln Institute published a research paper on America's vacant urban land.[35] This document concluded that land of this type is ubiquitous in American cities, which both poses a problem and supplies a potent resource for city governments. The paper also stated that these properties rapidly increase in cities with population growth due to past development practices that consumed more land per capita. That is, the in-between grows proportionately to population growth. Although, perhaps counterintuitive at first, the finding becomes less puzzling when one realizes that population density decreases as people spread to occupy greater land areas relative to population size.[36] Increasingly sprawl looks not just problematic, but inevitable given the dynamics of urban growth.

[33] Dorion Sagan and Eric D. Schneider, *Into The Cool: Energy Flow, Thermodynamics and Life* (Chicago: University of Chicago Press, 2005).
[34] See Christina Rosan, "Cleveland's Land Bank: Catalyzing a Renaissance in Affordable Housing," *Fannie Mae Foundation Housing Facts and Findings* 3, no.1 (2004). City of Cleveland Department of Communtiy Development for the Land Bank Database http://cd.city.cleveland.oh.us/scripts/db_details.php?db=landbank (accessed June 14, 2005).
[35] Bowman and Pagano, *Terra Incognita*. J. Bonham, Spilka Blaine, Gerri, Darl Rastorfer, *Old Cities/Green Cities: Communities Transform Unmanaged Land*, Planning Advisory Service Report no. 506/507 (Chicago: American Planning Association, 2002).
[36] Bowman and Pagano, *Terra Incognita*, 30.

Holey Planes and Stimdross

One of the most interesting manifestos written about urbanism over the past two decades is by Lars Lerup. His seminal 1995 essay, "Stim & Dross," has influenced the ways in which a generation of designers thinks about urbanization.[37] Using the city of Houston, as his example, Lerup theorizes over the city's vast stretch of urbanized landscape surface as a "holey plane" (the holes being voids in the urban plane): "This *holey plane* seems more a wilderness than a datum of a man-made city. Dotted by trees and criss-crossed by women/vehicles/roads, it is a surface dominated by a peculiar sense of ongoing struggle: the struggle of economics against nature. Both the trees and machines of this plane emerge as the (trail or) dross of that struggle."[38] Breaking from pro- and anti-sprawl rhetoric, Lerup momentarily suspended judgment in order to understand the forces creating the horizontal city. Lerup's stance presents an opportunity for designers to newly engage urbanization.

13—Downtown Cleveland, Ohio
The City of Cleveland employs an aggressive land bank program to adaptively redevelop inner city real estate.

> …the voids of the holey plane are clearly systematic, essential, and, as it may prove, fortuitous components of the ubiquitous American real estate machine…. Leapfrogged, these voids are elastic blobs that allow developers to hang onto their profit margins. The size and shape of the blob may in fact be a complex reflection of the dynamics of land costs, market forces, building practices, and peculiarities of local conditions…. Either way, these voids—a form of unintentional land-banking—are restored to a new potential.[39]

Lerup's holey plane is particularly useful for understanding relationships between landscape and urbanization. It reconceptualizes the city as a living, massive, dynamic system, or a huge ecological envelope of systematically productive and wasteful landscapes.[40] Innovating a more inclusive language for urbanization, Lerup exclaims: "Pools of cooled air dot the plane, much like oases In the desert. Precariously pinned in place by machines and human events, these pools become points of stimulation—stims—on this otherwise rough but uninflected hide, populated only by the dross—the ignored, undervalued, unfortunate economic residues of the metropolitan machine."[41] In other words, the urbanized landscape surface consists of two things: stim and dross. Stim characterizes the places, buildings, programs, and events that most people would identify as being developed or built for human use (dwelling, occupation, industry, recreation, etc.). Dross characterizes the landscape leftovers, or waste landscapes, typically found in-between the stims and undervalued for many reasons (pollution, vacancy, natural conditions unsuitable for building, unprofitability, etc.). Plugging in Lerup's terms—dross can be seen to be what I have been calling the "in-between" of a city's urban fabric.

[37] Lars Lerup, "Stim & Dross: Rethinking the Metropolis," *Assemblage 25* (Cambridge: MIT Press, 1995): 88.
[38] Ibid.
[39] Lars Lerup, *After the City* (Cambridge: MIT Press, 2000), 78.
[40] Ibid., 59. See also Lerup, "Stim & Dross," 83–100.
[41] Lerup, *After the City*, 58.

Fractals are another way to think about the holey plane. Today's urbanization is unique, whereby city and country penetrate one another, each having bits of the other within its borders. These bits and pieces shrink and grow through cyclical, irreversible processes. They are always determinately nonlinear. They never reach equilibrium (their cause and effect are unclear).[42] Thus, landscapes of the horizontal city move toward a richly complex mixture of city and country. The seemingly incoherent and chaotic landscape, however, is not passive. It is not just an ad hoc series of points, lines, patches, corridors, and edges.[43] While the city's visual appearance seems disorderly, its physical presence is ordered by the need to produce dross as it grows. Dross is a natural component of every dynamically evolving city. This book's underlying premise and guiding thesis is that as the world's landscape becomes increasingly urbanized, it is naturally saturated with dross (see figure 14).

Reflecting on Lerup's theory raises questions about what qualifies as dross. How would one describe

14—Ontario/Fontana area, California, about forty miles west of Los Angeles
Dross, a natural component of every city, increases with urban growth.

[42] Ilya Prigogene, *The End of Certainty* (New York: The Free Press, 1996), 64.
[43] For landscape ecology's use of these terms, see Wenche Dramstad, James Olson and Richard T.T. Forman, *Landscape Ecology Principles in Landscape Architecture and Land-Use Planning* (Cambridge, MA: Harvard University Graduate School of Design, Island Press, and the American Society of Landscape Architects, 1996); also see Forman, *Land Mosaics*. Stan Allen, *Points + Lines* (New York: Princeton Architectural Press, 1999), which interprets Forman's "landscape ecology" for infrastructural and architectural considerations.

an urban nature reserve? Does such a place qualify as stim or dross? If an urbanized landscape surface is intentionally designed (by an architect, planner, landscape architect, developer, politician, etc.) not to be activated, can it be considered dross? Lerup proposes reconceptualizing the city's surface as the hybrid field of "stimdross."[44] Finding a hybridization area where the attributes of stim and dross overlap (such as the urban nature reserve mentioned earlier or a property that is intentionally left vacant) becomes imperative for refining and testing his hypothesis. By definition, other possible stimdross includes derelict, polluted, abandoned industrial land and structures left uninhabited because of liability and remediation cost issues; it includes staging grounds or surfaces used (or not used) temporarily, as well as many other types of urbanized surface purposefully deprogrammed, underprogrammed, or voided of program (see figure 15). At the risk of oversimplifying Lerup's thesis, theorizing upon these hybridization areas proves much easier than finding them on the ground because locating "planned" dross requires knowing the intentions of the property owner, and arguably, the larger market forces affecting the land. This information cannot be found solely through visual observation. As the images in this book attest, economic and geographic research must go hand-in-hand with visual observation in order to know what lies behind the picture.

15—Highlands Ranch, Colorado, Douglas County
Some urbanized surfaces are purposefully deprogrammed, underprogrammed, or voided of program. The sign reads: "Future Highlands Ranch Historic Park and Other Allowed Uses."

From In-Between to Freedom and Waste

The problem that is usually being visualized is how capitalism administers existing structures, whereas the relevant problem is how it creates and destroys them.
–Joseph Schumpeter, *Capitalism, Socialism and Democracy*

Future urban infill and growth depend on salvaging and re-imagining the collective body of in-between landscapes. For many American cities, as landscape surfaces accumulate through horizontal urbanization, it becomes paramount to locate waste and identify potential problems and opportunities for reusing it.

As revealed in recent history, public perception can be manipulated and manufactured (to create and pass referenda and balloting measures) to fund public and private urban infill projects like sporting-event facilities, libraries, museums, etc., with public tax revenues.[45] Voters consistently approve new funding mechanisms for infrastructural improvements such as buildings, roadway widening, school construction, and flood-control/sewer projects. Conversely, they often disapprove of tax increases earmarked for urban

[44] Lars Lerup, *After the City*, 62.
[45] Raymond Keating, "Sports Pork: The Costly Relationship Between Major League Sports and Government," *Cato Policy Analysis*, no. 339 (Washington, DC: Cato Institute, 1999). Since the early 1990s, fourteen new Major League Baseball stadia have been built with at least three more under construction. Upon completion, seventeen of the thirty Major League Baseball teams will be playing in stadia built since 1992. The National Football League has seventeen of thirty-two teams playing in stadia built since 1992, once those currently under construction are completed. It is estimated that approximately $10 billion of public money has gone to all new sports stadia since the mid 1980s. Also see Kevin J. Delaney and Rick Eckstein, *Public Dollars, Private Stadiums: The Battle over Building Sports Stadiums* (Piscataway, N.J.: Rutgers University Press, 2003).

landscape improvements.[46] These are typically left to the workings of the private-sector or existing city-department budgets (such as Parks and Recreation) or piggybacked on engineering projects.

This points to the fact that there is resistance surrounding the legitimacy of publicly funded improvements to in-between landscape. Pro- and anti-sprawl as well as conservation advocates may serve as examples of this phenomenon. Both constituencies try to extinguish the existence of the in-between landscape. The mission of pro-sprawl constituencies is to develop as much land as possible (or as much as the market demands). Conversely, the mission of anti-sprawl constituencies is to conserve as much land and open space as possible. Both groups use private funding to achieve their landscape missions.

In terms of the urban landscape a consensus on what one considers in-between is improbable. This is because the definition of waste is at issue. Americans consciously choose the types of waste landscape they value. This decision is highly personal. The issue evokes arguments of individual freedom and liberty. The International Society for Individual Liberty (ISL), for example, developed the world's largest libertarian portal to the Internet to discuss, in part, environmental topics. One of the ISL's services is Free-Market.net, which contains free-market analyses and literature on urban sprawl.

It is largely produced by independent, conservative research institutes and other think tanks. One can find a variety of libertarian arguments that link issues of waste, landscape, city form, and individual liberties (see table 1).[47] These groups support market-oriented alternatives to conventional urban-development and planning policy in contrast to traditional forms of government intervention and controls. Any legislation controlling urban growth, in the libertarian view, compromises individual freedom as well as the values that formed and galvanized America's founding principles.

Waste was long regarded as part of urbanization. For example, cities as diverse as ancient Rome and Manhattan dumped garbage, bones, and all matter of debris from daily life into the streets as a means of disposing trash while physically elevating the city. In older cities, people live on top of their waste.[48] Today, of course, there are requirements for appropriate fill materials and most solid municipal wastes are dumped in landfills outside populated areas. Water is treated in specialized sewage-treatment plants (see figures 16, 17). After World War II, the production of waste became associated with social processes of freedom,

Table 1
Links to organizations providing literature, linking waste, city form, and individual liberties
Independence Institute www.i2i.org
Pacific Research Institute www.pacificresearch.org
Political Economy Research Center www.perc.org
National Center for Public Policy Research www.ncppr.org
Reason Public Policy Institute www.rppi.org
Goldwater Institute www.goldwaterinstitute.org
Cato Institute www.cato.org
Competitive Enterprise Institute www.cei.org
Resources for the Future www.rff.org
Heartland Institute www.heartland.org
Heritage Foundation www.heritage.org
Georgia Public Policy Foundation www.gppf.org
Mackinac Center for Public Policy www.mackinac.org
Texas Public Policy Foundation www.texaspolicy.org
Thoreau Institute www.ti.org
Wendell Cox Consultancy www.publicpurpose.com
Buckeye Institute www.buckeyeinstitute.org
Planning and Markets www-pam.usc.edu
Cascade Policy Institute www.cascadepolicy.org
Small Business Survival Committee www.sbsc.org
Demographia www.demographia.com

[46] Valerie Alvord, "State Parks Squeezed, Shut by Budget Woes," *USA Today*, July 24, 2002; Kristen Mack, "Police, Fire Departments New Budget's Bid Winners," *Houston Chronicle*, May 21, 2004; Ralph Ranalli, "Funding Urged to Preserve Ecology," *Boston Globe*, March 31, 2005, B1, B6; Stephan Lovgren, "U.S. National Parks Told to Quietly Cut Services," *National Geographic News*, March 19, 2004, http://news.nationalgeographic.com/news/2004/03/0319_040319_parks.html (accessed May 10, 2005).
[47] Wendell Cox, "Debunking Friday the 13th: 13 Myths of Urban Sprawl," *News Releases*, (Chicago: The Heartland Institute, June 12, 2003), http://www.heartland.org/Article.cfm?artId=12350 (accessed June 19, 2003).
[48] William Rathje and Cullen Murphy, *Rubbish: The Archeology of Garbage* (Tuscon, AZ: University of Arizona Press, 2001), 34–35.

power, and convenience.[49] According to historian Susan Strasser, "Disposable products, food packaging, and the convenience, cleanliness, and labor savings they represented were understood to distinguish the freedom of modernity from the drudgery of old-fashioned life."[50]

Travel to any American urbanized area, and you will find "wastefulness" in many forms. Might this reveal the values of the people who live and govern there? Just like physical waste, what is considered "wasteful" is deeply embedded in a culture's value system. Americans carefully choose the ways they weave wastefulness, inefficiencies, and excesses—or the opposites—into their lives. As a result, cultural preferences and environmental ethics play larger and larger roles in the structuring of cities.[51] The recent ascension of the politically correct slogan "sustainability," or more precisely, "sustainable development" is an example. How one determines that a condition is sustainable has everything to do with local values and context. Someone living in a developing country, for example, would not define sustainability on the same ethical grounds as someone living in a highly industrialized nation. Moreover, it has been

16—Landfill near Kirtland, Ohio, about twenty-five miles east of Cleveland
Most solid municipal wastes are dumped in landfill operations outside of populated areas.

[49] Susan Strasser, *Waste and Want: A Social History of Trash* (New York: Henry Holt and Company, 1999), 9, 266–68.
[50] Ibid., 268.
[51] Georges Bataille, *The Accursed Share, Volume 1: Consumption*, trans. Robert Hurley (reprint ed., New York: Zone Books, 1991). Bataille develops the idea of a "general economy" based on waste and excess energy from the sun rather than having and hoarding. Also see Mira Engler, *Designing America's Waste Landscapes* (Baltimore: Johns Hopkins University Press, 2004).

17—Water treatment plant along the Salt River
outside of Phoenix, Arizona
Municipal wastewater is treated in specialized
sewage treatment plants. This facility is located
on the periphery of urban Phoenix.

argued that sustainable development is nothing more
than an excuse created by rich, developed countries
to further impoverish poorer nations.[52] Regardless of
one's moral or ethical position on sustainability, it is
clear that issues of consumption and waste are not based
on homogeneous value systems, but rather on local,
contextual doxa, and praxis. The result is that multitudes
of "waste" spread unevenly in numerous ways throughout
the landscape.

With regards to "waste," it is impossible to isolate
re-characterizations of the city from its socioeconomic
milieu. Horizontal urbanization results in part from what,
in 1942, Harvard University economist Joseph Schumpeter
called "The Process of Creative Destruction."[53] Schumpeter
believed that innovations made by entrepreneurs began
with this process, which relegated old inventories,
technologies, equipment, and even craftsmen's skills to
obsolescence.[54] From this one can derive a contemporary
reading of the horizontal city's in-between landscape,
Lerup's dross, as a palimpsest of waste leftover from
creative destruction. Lerup's stim and dross is the physical
cognate for creative destruction. These terms acknowledge
the totality of the consumption-waste cycle and the

[52] Wilfred Beckerman, *A Poverty of Reason: Sustainable Development and
Economic Growth* (Oakland, CA: The Independent Institute, 2003), 64–66.
[53] Joseph A. Schumpeter, *Capitalism, Socialism and Democracy,* 3rd ed.
(New York: Harper & Row Publishers, 1950), 81–110. See also Sharon Zukin,
Landscapes of Power (Berkeley, CA: University of California Press, 1991), 41.
Zukin describes Schumpeter's "creative destruction" as a "liminal"
landscape, thus bringing my discussion of a liminal landscape full circle.
[54] Schumpeter, *Capitalism, Socialism and Democracy,* 84.

organic integration of waste into the urban world as the
result of socioeconomic processes (see figure 18).

Other theories have been posited over the past
century concerning relationships between waste and
economic production. The key to economic achievement
is to spend and consume.[55] So stated J. George Frederick,
president of the Business Bourse publishing house, and
his wife, Christine Frederick, a prominent home economist
and advertising consultant more than a decade prior to
Schumpeter's "creative destruction" thesis. They coined
the phrases "progressive obsolescence" and "creative
waste." Progressive obsolescence essentially means that
the new business of industrialization is founded on the
principle of wasting things before they are completely
used or worn out. A similar idea was promoted by
President George W. Bush, after the 9/11 terrorist attacks
under the guise of creating economic stimulus: "We need
to stimulate the economy through boosting consumer
confidence with some kind of money in the hands of
consumers."[56] Strasser notes that economically driven
accumulation creates waste whether through consumer
goods (raw consumption) or by the ways we choose to live

18—Downtown Dallas, Texas
The new housing development lays on former
industrial land. This example depicts the
completion of the consumption/waste cycle.
Organic integration of waste is a natural, as well
as a socio-economic, process in city-making.

[55] J. Frederick George, *A Philosophy of Production* (New York: The
Business Bourse, 1930), 227. See Also Roland Marchand, *Advertising
the American Dream* (Berkeley, CA: University of California Press, 1986),
156. Also see Susan Strasser, *Waste and Want: A Social History of Trash*
(New York: Henry Holt and Company, 1999), 198.
[56] White House Office of the Press Secretary, "President Works on
Economic Recovery During NY Trip," press release, October 3, 2001 at
http://www.whitehouse.gov/news/releases/2001/10/20011003-4.html
(accessed December 9, 2004).

(freedom): "Trash and trashmaking became integral to the economy in a wholly new way: the growth of markets for new products came to depend in part on the continuous disposal of old things."[57] Today an entire field of study is devoted to understanding the social and environmental implications of waste and the industrial past. Two such organizations are the Society for Industrial Archeology, with some 1,800 members world wide, and the University of Arizona's Garbage Project, which, over the past several decades, has been studying the archaeology of garbage by using data, digging through landfills, and analyzing solid-waste streams.[58]

Coda: Urban Landscape is a Natural Thing to Waste

Films such as Koyaanisqatsi and Baraka image the city from aerial overviews and via time-lapse photography in such a way as to reveal their strikingly organism-like aspects. The city is ultimately a natural process whose unperceived complexity cannot be completely controlled and planned.[59]

The situation is not unlike that of living organisms, whose hard parts, from the bones and shells of terrestrial vertebrates and marine invertebrates to the iron and other elements and compounds precipitated by cells, originated in the expelling and/or managing of wastes. Calcium, for example, used for that living infrastructure of the human body, the skeleton, is routinely extruded by cells in the marine environment; this striking example is not an analogy, but arguably a homology for how waste becomes incorporated into landscape structure and function. The economies that provide the energy and materials for the growth of cities, such as manufacturing output and housing starts, are not so much things as processes. And, as is true for organisms, the faster they grow the more (potentially hazardous) waste they produce. This is a natural process that can be ignored, maligned, or embraced, but never stopped. "What is now emerging is an 'intermediate' description [of reality] that lies somewhere between the two alienating images of a deterministic world and an arbitrary world of pure chance,"[60] wrote Nobel Laureate Ilya Prigogine. These words, regarding the unpredictability of complex systems, apply perfectly to the realm of landscapes in urbanization. Cities are not static structures, but active arenas marked by continuous energy flows and transformations of which landscapes and physical buildings and other parts are not permanent but transitional structures. Like a biological organism, the urbanized landscape is an open system, whose planned complexity always entails unplanned dross. To expect a planned city to function without waste (such as in a cradle to cradle approach), which represents the

[57] Strasser, *Waste and Want*, 15.
[58] Rathje and Murphy, *Rubbish*.
[59] *Koyaanisqatsi: Life Out of Balance*, is an independent film by Francis Ford Coppola, Godfrey Reggio, and The Institute for Regional Education. Created between 1975 and 1982, the film is an apocalyptic vision of the collision of urban life and technology with the natural environment. *Baraka* (1992) directed by Ron Fricke, uses breathtaking shots from around the world to show the beauty and destruction of nature and humans.
[60] Ilya Prigogine, *The End of Certainty* (New York: The Free Press, 1996), 189.

in situ or exported excess not only of its growth but of its maintenance, is as naïve as expecting an animal to thrive in a sensory deprivation tank. The challenge for designers is thus not to achieve drossless urbanization, but to integrate inevitable dross into more flexible aesthetic and design strategies.

With these ideas in the conceptual background my goal is to link together the practical and theoretical issues concerning urbanization and dross to make associations among industrial, economic, and consumption activity and the landscapes created as a result of these processes. Contemporary modes of industrial production, driven by economical and consumerist influences, contribute to urbanization and the formation of "waste landscapes"–meaning actual *waste* (such as municipal solid waste, sewage, scrap metal, etc.), *wasted* places (such as abandoned and/or contaminated sites), or *wasteful* places (such as huge parking lots, retail malls, etc.). The term *urban sprawl* and the rhetorics of pro- and anti-urban sprawl advocates all but obsolesce under the realization that there is no growth without waste and that urban growth and dross go hand in hand, and always have, not because of anything human, or indeed even pertaining to life, but due to physics itself. Complex processes must export waste to their boundaries in order to maintain and grow. This is the lesson that designers of the built environment should learn from nonequilibrium thermodynamics; and it is one we need not belabor but which must be incorporated as an assumption into our understanding of landscape in urbanization.

Chapter Two
The Production of Waste Landscape

We are shifting not out of industry into services, but from one
kind of industrial economy to another.
–Stephen Cohen and John Zysman, *Manufacturing Matters:
The Myth of the Post-Industrial Economy*

Deindustrialization:
Waste Landscape Through Attrition

America is deindustrializing. Since 1990 more than
600,000 abandoned and contaminated waste sites have
been identified within American cities.[1] How did this
waste landscape come to be? What will we do with it?
How will it affect urbanizing areas in the future? Who
is best qualified to deal with the abundance of waste
landscape? Controversial questions like these are difficult
to answer. This subject has produced some of the late
twentieth century's most debated bodies of scholarship.[2]
A book such as this cannot definitively answer these
questions. It can and does, however, address the topic
of deindustrialization in the context of the relationships
between landscape and urbanization. As America rapidly
deindustrializes, it is simultaneously urbanizing faster
than at any other time in modern history. What then are
the links between urbanization, deindustrialization and
the production of waste landscape in American cities?

Designers often paint a black-and-white picture
of complex industrial processes. The most commonly
used term, *postindustrial*, has been used both spatially
and formalistically to describe everything from polluted
industrial landscapes to former factory buildings, usually
found in older, declining sections of a city.[3] The term
itself, *postindustrial*, arguably creates as many [or
more] problems than solutions in rethinking landscapes
leftover from previous industrial eras. The reason for this
may be that the concept of the postindustrial narrowly
isolates and objectifies the landscape as being the
result of very specific processes that no longer operate
upon a given site (residual pollution aside). This outlook
reifies the site as essentially static and in isolation and
defines it in terms of a pre-industrial past rather than as
an ongoing industrial process that forms other parts

[1] "$76.7 Million in Brownfield Grants Announced," May 10, 2005, and "EPA
Announces $73.1 Million in National Brownfields Grants in 37 States and
Seven Tribal Communities," June 20, 2003, U.S. EPA Brownfield official web
site http://www.epa.gov/brownfields/archive/pilot_arch.htm (accessed
May 21, 2005); Niall Kirkwood, "Why is There So Little Residential
Redevelopment on Brownfields? Framing Issues for Discussion," paper
W01-3, *Joint Center for Housing Studies*, (Cambridge, MA: Harvard
University, January 2001), 3–4.
[2] Daniel Bell, *The Coming of Post-Industrial Society* (New York: Basic Books,
1999); Barry Bluestone and Bennett Harrison, *The Deindustrialization of
America* (New York: Basic Books, 1982); Stephen Cohen and John Zysman,
Manufacturing Matters: The Myth of the Post-Industrial Economy (New
York: Basic Books, 1987); Michael J. Piore and Charles F. Sabel, *The Second
Industrial Divide* (New York: Basic Books, 1984).
[3] My use of this term *postindustrial* here and in other publications, does
not imply that industrial production and/or industrial-induced land
alteration has stopped. I suggest that a new condition exists that shifts
industrial production toward technology and away from mechanics,
leaving vacant and contaminated mechanical-industrial sites in its
wake. There is no break from "industrial" to "post-industrial" landscape
formation, only a shift in industrial-landscape types.

of the city. There are many examples of this outlook that manifest in the redesigning of industrial production sites for reuse.[4] I suggest that it would be strategically helpful in the short-term to suspend the term postindustrial and its value system when discussing the city.

In their book, *The Myth of the Post-Industrial Landscape*, Stephen Cohen and John Zysman argue that the term postindustrial society captures our imagination and is a way of seeing the world, but may not be a real thing. They conclude that there has never been nor will there ever be a postindustrial society. They argue: "The division of labor has become infinitely more elaborate and the production process far more indirect.... But the key generator of wealth for this vastly expanded and differentiated division of labor remains mastery and control of production. We are shifting not out of industry into services, but from one-kind of industrial economy to another."[5]

Deindustrialization is most interesting if it's considered in terms of production and geography. According to the AFL-CIO, industrialized areas in the U.S. have lost more than 285,000 manufacturing jobs since March of 1998. This has accelerated deindustrialization in a broad array of industries, from steel, textiles, apparel, automobiles, and electronics to aerospace: "No region has escaped the ravages of the crisis."[6] Post–World War II sentiment against "dirty" industries in favor of "clean" businesses such as offices, banks, and brokerages led to public policy that also catalyzed urban industrial attrition. No clearer example persists than in New York City. Manufacturing jobs fell from almost 1 million in the 1950s to about two hundred thousand in 2001.[7] Fulton County, the central county comprising the city of Atlanta, Georgia, experienced more than a 26 percent decrease in manufacturing establishments from 1977 to 2001, while outlying counties (some seventy miles away from the center of Atlanta) experienced more than 300 percent growth in this sector (see Chapter 3).[8]

Manufacturing in America, as in much of the developed world, is decentralized. It takes fewer people located in one central place to make the same or more product than it did in the past. Laborwise, manufacturing employment continues to shrink as efficiency gains make it possible to augment output, thanks to automation and global outsourcing (see figures 19, 20). From 1979 to 1989 manufacturing employment in the U.S. declined from more than 21 million to 19.4 million, despite the recovery in the U.S. economy. From 1989 to 1999 manufacturing employment shrank even further to

[4] See various contemporary examples of this approach and outlook in Kirkwood, *Manufactured Sites*.
[5] Cohen and Zysman, *Manufacturing Matters*, 26.
[6] AFL-CIO Executive Council Actions, "Trade and Deindustrialization," February 18, 1999, http://www.aflcio.org/aboutaflcio/ecouncil/ec02181999a.cfm (accessed June 19, 2001). Also see Oliver Gillham, *The Limitless City* (Washington, DC: Island Press, 2002), 39-40.
[7] Roger Doyle, "Deindustrialization: Why Manufacturing Continues to Decline," *ScientificAmerican.com*, March 22 Issue, http://www.sciam.com/article.cfm?articleID=00094F4E-11F8-1CD4-B4A8809EC588EEDF&sc=I100322 (accessed June 14, 2005).
[8] U.S. Census Bureau State and County Quickfacts, 1998; Georgia Business QuickLinks, http://quickfacts.census.gov/qfd/states/13000lk.html, and Georgia County Business Patterns Economic Profile, 1997, and 2001,http://www.census.gov/epcd/cbp/map/01data/13/999.txt (both accessed July 22, 2004).

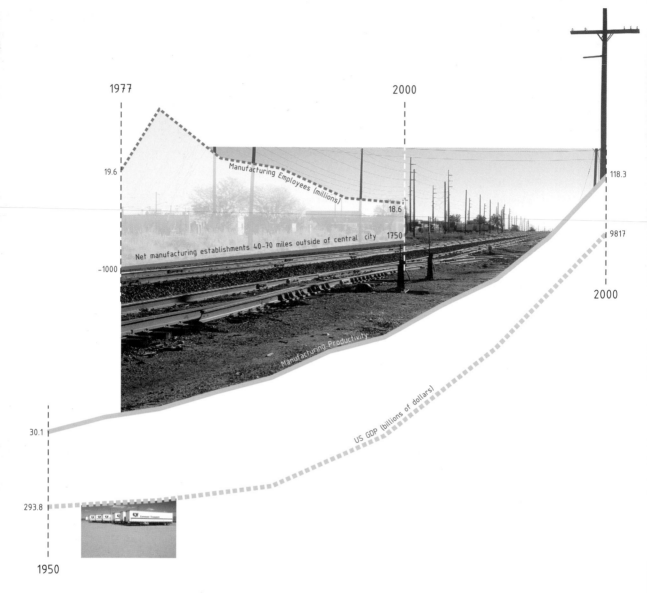

1977   2000

19.6   Manufacturing Employees (millions)   118.3

18.6

Net manufacturing establishments 40-70 miles outside of central city   1750   9817

-1000   2000

Manufacturing Productivity

30.1   US GDP (billions of dollars)

293.8

1950

18.6 million, even as full recovery materialized. During the 2001–02 recession, manufacturing employment fell to 16.5 million. Going all the way back to 1959, 31.2 percent or nearly one third of U.S. workers were in manufacturing. In 2001 they numbered 12.6 percent.[9]

While manufacturing trends are key indicators for industrial transformations, job creation or destruction does not tell the entire story of deindustrialization. For instance, it reveals how industrial evolution alters the landscape of the city.[10] Its broadest meanings are derived from the history of capitalism and evolving patterns of investment and disinvestment.[11] The city itself is considered a product of industrialization (capital and production flows), that does not simply begin or end, but evolves to affect city form and function in various ways.

For much of the late-eighteenth and nineteenth centuries the American city landscape was designed and

19—Manufacturing Productivity in the U.S.
From 1977 to 2000 manufacturing employment in the U.S. declined from more than 19.6 million to 18.6 million. During this period there has been a large net increase in manufacturing establishments located in outlying areas some forty to seventy miles from their respective central cities.

[9] Jefferson Cowie and Jospeh Heathcott, eds. *Beyond the Ruins: The Meanings of Deindustrialization* (Ithaca: Cornell University Press, 2003), xii. Also see Council of Economic Advisers, *Economic Report of the President*, 1998, U.S. Government Printing Office, http://www.gpoaccess.gov/eop/; and Council of Economic Advisers, *Economic Indicators*, January 2003, U.S. Government Printing Office at http://www.gpoaccess.gov/indicators/.
[10] Cowie and Heathcott, *Beyond the Ruins*, 14.
[11] Ibid., 15.

built to represent a view opposite to those developed by industrialization. The professions of landscape architecture and urban planning were influenced by anti-industrialization offerings. Three seminal designers of the late-nineteenth and twentieth centuries promoted the use of landscape as a means to counter the environmentally and socially destructive impact of the industrialized city. Their landscapes were designed and invested in as a respite from urban congestion and the pollution created by industrialization. Ebenezer Howard's "garden cities" of the late nineteenth century were planned with integrated road and railway networks. They were intended to promote and sustain decentralization of older cities and the creation of garden cities on the perimeter of congested production zones. Frank Lloyd Wright's plan for Broadacre City, designed in the 1920s, envisioned universal car ownership as inevitable. The plan, therefore, provided for an ever-extending grid of public highways to support a shift toward decentralization, sustainability, and progressive abandonment of the big, "obsolete" industrial city. Le Corbusier's plan for the Radiant City proposed to replace the old, chaotic industrial city with a "rationalized urban landscape." It was to be composed of clean, modern interconnections and land-use separations. The quintessential example of this line of thinking evolved during the City Beautiful movement (1900–10), as middle-class citizens attempted to transform their cities into beautiful, functional places after the Industrial Revolution.

Arguably, the result of such approaches is a net increase in the amount of waste landscape in cities.

20—Global III Intermodal Terminal, Rochelle, Illinois, about eighty miles west of Chicago
Union Pacific Railroad's facility was completed in 2003. It features a ten-lane automated gate system and processes over 7,200 containers daily.

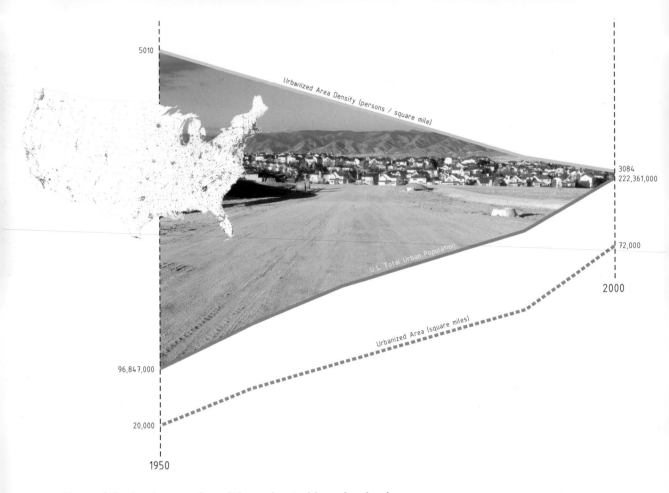

5010

Urbanized Area Density (persons / square mile)

3084
222,361,000

72,000

2000

U.S. Total Urban Population

Urbanized Area (square miles)

96,847,000

20,000

1950

Many of the landscapes found throughout older urbanized areas are manifestations of previous anti-urban attitudes associated with industrialization. Urban populations continue to decentralize and the dense city is no longer the hub of industrial activity. As the result of fewer constituents, "respite" landscapes in many inner cities are now in severe decline and disinvestment (see figure 21). Thirty states in 2004 operated with frozen or reduced Parks and Recreation budgets. Currently hundreds of state parks are closed or operate for fewer hours with reduced services, such as maintenance, in order to remain fiscally solvent.[12] In 2003 California's Department of Parks and Recreation, the nation's largest with 274 parks, raised entrance fees to compensate for a $35 million budget cut. Roughly $600 million is still needed for deferred maintenance projects.[13] The U.S. National Park Service also seeks private-sector support for park maintenance in the face of staffing shortages and budget cutbacks of billions of dollars.[14]

21—Urban Land Density in the U.S.
From 1950 to 2000 urbanized area density (persons per square mile) has decreased by more than 50 percent.

[12] Alvord, *USA Today;* Ralph Ranalli, *Boston Globe*; Also see "2004 Chicago Park District Budget Crisis, Park Advocates Requests" at Chicago's Hyde Park-Kenwood Community Conference Parks Committee (HPKCC) web site, http://www.hydepark.org/parks/04budcrisisreqs.htm (accessed June 14, 2005); Mike Tobin and Angela Townsend, "Budget Assumes Flat Economy," *The Plain Dealer*, January 28, 2004, http://www.cleveland.com/budgetcrisis/index.ssf?/budgetcrisis/more/1075285840190290.html (accessed June 14, 2005).
[13] Ibid. Also see Joy Lanzendorfer, "Parks and Wreck," *North Bay Bohemian*, July 3–9, 2003. Project for Public Spaces is an organization that campaigns against landscape budget, http://www.pps.org. A much different picture of open space funding is depicted by the Trust for Public Land. See their LandVote Database, http://www.tpl.org/tier2_kad.cfm?content_item_id=0&folder_id=2607 (accessed June 14, 2005), which reveals that the majority of the ballot measures for the "conservation" of open space have passed over the last decade.
[14] For national parks, see Stephan Lovgren, *National Geographic News*; Geoffrey Cantrell, "Critics Fear Park Service Headed Down Wrong Path," *Boston Globe*, March 10, 2005.

For the past four decades American industrial production has been undergoing an imperceptible relocation from traditional downtown cores to the urban periphery, and even to other countries. This mass exodus from older urban, industrialized areas changes the physical appearance of cities. It creates a serious economic impact for cities now forced to compete with newer urbanizing areas for the public funding needed to maintain deteriorating inner-city landscapes and infrastructures. Together deindustrialization, decentralization, and horizontal urbanization are the largest factor for land vacancy in large American cities during the 1990s.[15]

Deindustrialization is not homogeneous: it has affected every major city in the U.S. in varying ways (see figure 22), some of which are positive. Deindustrialization creates new employment opportunities; the plight of industrial workers has been an economic boon to other businesses. Mike Davis describes the deindustrialization of Los Angeles in *Dead Cities*:

22—Deindustrialized landscape in Collinwood, Ohio
In 1999 the Ohio EPA created its Voluntary Action Program aimed at cleaning up contaminated properties and returning them to productive use. Some 11,400 acres of urban commercial and industrial property, containing more than 14,000 sites in the Cleveland region will be redeveloped as a result of this program.

> Unlike Detroit or Youngstown, LA's derelict industrial core was not simply abandoned. Almost as fast as Fortune 500 corporations shut down their LA branch plants, local capitalists rushed in to take advantage of the Southeast's cheap leases, tax incentives, and burgeoning supply of immigrant Mexican labor…. Within the dead shell of heavy manufacturing, a new sweatshop economy emerged.
>
> The old Firestone Rubber and American Can plants, for instance, have been converted into nonunion furniture factories, while the great Bethlehem Steel Works on Slauson Avenue has been replaced by a hot-dog distributor, a Chinese food-products company, and a maker of rattan patio furniture. Chrysler Maywood is now a bank "back office," while US Steel has metamorphosed into a warehouse complex, and the "Assyrian" wall of Uniroyal Tire has become a facade for a designer-label outlet center.[16]

All deindustrialized sites are not equal. Some find new life immediately by filling an economic niche, such as the immigrant labor force in Los Angeles, or by filling a cultural niche, such as the California Speedway in Fontana (see figure 23). Others are immediately cordoned off due to severe contamination. Many others are left abandoned for decades until market forces or technological innovation produce resources for their rehabilitation (see figure 24). Imperatively, deindustrialized sites are all transitional places. They await some form of reclamation prior to reprogramming and reuse. Another characteristic they have in common is their pedigree: they were previously active industrial sites, located in close proximity to densely populated urban areas. Optimistically, it could

[15]Bowman and Pagano, *Terra Incognita*, 12.
[16]Davis, *Dead Cities*, 193.

be argued that as deindustrialization proliferates and as industry relocates from central cities to peripheral areas, America's cities will enjoy a net gain in the total landscapes (and buildings) available for other uses.[17] Changes in manufacturing and production and modes of communication and transportation have resulted in the dispersal and relocation of industrial production to outlying areas and beyond. Deindustrialization creates waste landscape through the attrition of industrial landscapes and buildings in the older parts of the traditional central city. Adaptively reusing this waste landscape figures to be one of the twenty-first century's great infrastructural design challenges as these sites are potentially transformable into new productive uses such as permanent open landscapes or infill developments.

23—California Speedway, Fontana, California, about forty-five miles west of Los Angeles, San Bernardino County (opposite, top)
The speedway exists on land formerly occupied by a steel mill. Fabricated metal products and other manufacturing activities surround the site.

24—Alameda Corridor, Los Angeles, California (opposite, bottom)
Many deindustrialized landscapes are cordoned off due to severe contamination. Some sites are left abandoned for decades until market forces or technological innovation creates resources for their rehabilitation.

Post-Fordism: Waste Landscape Through Accumulation
Cities are not just sites of production, they are also important sites of consumption.
–Michael Storper, *The Regional World*

Flexibility
Fordist systems of mass production fueled the organization of cities from the early 1900s to 1950s. The Fordist city stressed automation, standardization, economies of scale, and the technical division of labor communication, all supported by hierarchically organized infrastructures. Fordism's spatial translation is found in the modernist ideals of city making and masterplanning. Geographically, Fordism operated by centralizing production and management into a single, large complex that produced all the components and assembled the product on site. Fordism also references means of consumption and accumulation. The Fordist regime of accumulation, for example, describes a social and economic organization supported by a set of production and regulatory mechanisms geared toward production for an ever-expanding homogeneous mass consumer market. The prototypical Fordist city was designed with respite landscapes to counter its environmentally and socially deleterious effects.

Flexibility is a term often used to describe the evolution from Fordist to post-Fordist economies and refers to the organization of labor or production methods that can adjust easily to changing demands, consumption trends, and shifting markets, while avoiding the limitations of centralized mass production

[17] For example, see Philadelphia Neighborhood Transformation Initiative (NTI), http://www.phila.gov/nti/pressreleases05.htm (accessed June 14, 2005). Philadelphia reports: "In April 2001, the City of Philadelphia officially launched the Neighborhood Transformation Initiative (NTI), a multi-faceted, $300 million+ effort to improve the quality of life in all neighborhoods. Since then, under NTI the City has amassed a wide array of successes: more than 224,000 abandoned cars removed from its streets and 44,000 tons of debris cleared from 31,000 vacant lots; 23,000 dead trees cut down; 6,000 dangerous buildings demolished; and, at last count, more than 21,000 units of new housing, (either completed, planned or underway), to serve buyers or renters at all income levels–affordable, low income and market rate."

and the Fordist division of labor.[18] This flexibility is associated with what has been called post-Fordism. The post-Fordist process of production and consumption consists of flexible plants and labor that can cost-effectively produce smaller batches of more customized goods, which can rapidly change based on shifts in consumer demand. The demise of nuclear, dense, vertically ordered cities has been linked to the end of Fordism. Today many suggest that a series of concurrent post-Fordist socioeconomic conditions challenged the hierarchical city and that this eventually led to a series of "liquefying" spatio-economic patterns for business organization. These patterns are supported by extensive highway and infrastructure networks that allow production facilities to locate outside the traditional city while ensuring quick and efficient access to distribution hubs. Industries and businesses that locate in such a manner tend to cluster together and share customized networked infrastructures for their own internal purposes.[19] For example, dozens of automotive-parts suppliers agglomerated along a stretch of Interstate 85 in Spartanburg, South Carolina, after BMW established its North American production facility there in 1992. This area is part of the Southern Automotive Corridor, a multistate network of rail and highway infrastructural bundling specifically tailored to auto manufacturers.[20]

Flexible modes of production create more waste landscape. This is because either more firms or more capacity (meaning larger facilities) is needed to meet the real-time demands of customized production and fluctuating consumer tastes. Stephen Cohen and John Zysman, co-directors of the Berkeley Roundtable on the International Economy at the University of California at Berkeley, and co-authors of *Manufacturing Matters: The Myth of the Post-Industrial Economy*, state that there are competitive inefficiencies for large, flexible business firms: "In upturns, the contracts can be signed, and in downturns, canceled or not renewed. The small subcontractor then bears the costs of demand swings, rather than the large firm. The mix of production strategies allows firms to purchase flexibility. The price of flexibility is the difference between the cost of a product produced in the most efficient plant (at the plant's most efficient volume) and the cost of the same product produced in a different factory or bought from a subcontractor. Why use less efficient facilities? Because they provide capacity

25—Fort Worth/Alliance Airport, Alliance, Texas, about fourteen miles north of Fort Worth (above)
This airport is an 11,600-acre, master-planned international trade and logistics complex built for handling new, globalized, flexible manufacturing and distribution. It is a 100 percent industrial airport with intermodal hub facilities and Triple Freeport Inventory Tax Exemption and Foreign Trade Zone status.

[18] The term flexibility is derived from a concept called the "flexible regime of accumulation," which David Harvey and Allen Scott coined by bringing together Michel Aglietta's concept of the "Fordist regime of accumulation" that started with the French Regulation School and Flexible Specialization studies. David Harvey and Allen J. Scott, "The Practice of Human Geography, Theory and Specificity in the Transition from Fordist to Flexible Accumulation," *Remodeling Geography*, ed. W. Macmillan (Cambridge: Blackwell, 1988). Also see Michel Aglietta, *A Theory of Capitalist Regulation: The U.S. Experience*, trans. David Fernbach (London: New Left Books, 1979). For a synopsis of these ideas see Marco Cenzatti, "Industrial Districts and Urbane Restrukturierung," *Urban Form-Stadtebau in der Postfordistschen Gesellschaft*, eds. R. Banik-Schweitzer and E. Blau (Vienna: Locker, 2003). I also thank Marco Cenzatti for a personal conversation in Cambridge, Massachusetts, in April 2004.
[19] Graham and Marvin, *Splintering Urbanism*, 115. See also Alejandro Zaera Polo, "Order out of Chaos" *The Periphery, Architectural Design Profile no. 108*, eds. Jonathan Woodroffe, Dominic Papa, and Ian MacBurnie (London: Wiley/Architectural Design, 1994), 24–29.
[20] Southern Business & Development magazine official web site, http://www.southernautocorridor.com.

that can be closed off when demand drops, and because equipment is less dedicated and the facilities can be closed or turned to new uses. The firm is able to minimize production costs over time across a range of production volumes."[21] Flexible manufacturing creates the need for more facilities, buildings, roads, and sites and ultimately leads to more waste landscape (see figure 25).

Allen Scott, professor of geography at UCLA, asserts that the U.S. is in a post-Fordist urban economy. He provides another reading of flexibility.[22] He believes a city's economic base is made up of industries that need to "agglomerate" in districts outside the city core. The geographic ramifications of post-Fordism are very different from those of Fordism.[23]

Scott concludes that new territories are formed on the periphery of cities in order to accommodate flexible production.[24] He contends that there are regional differences in flexible activity, and that some places do a better job of competing in a flexible economy and consequently experience faster growth. The main Sunbelt states of Arizona, California, Florida, Georgia, and Texas exhibit the most rapidly growing peripheral spaces, created out of the flexible production methods of capitalization. These states specifically attempt to attract new industry by using tax incentives and planning policy. Phoenix, Arizona, offers income-tax and property-tax benefits to qualifying businesses located within the City of Phoenix Enterprise Zone (COPEZ). Businesses that qualify enter a Foreign Trade Zone (FTZ), in which they defer or eliminate the duty on goods imported to the U.S. As an indirect result of these and other economic-growth policies, the high-technology and aerospace industries in the Phoenix metropolitan region employ 30 percent of all local manufacturing workers, compared with the U.S. average of 10 percent.[25]

26—Intel's Ocotillo Campus, Chandler, Arizona
Phoenix and other Sunbelt cities are ripe for attracting flexible industries as they offer special economic and free trade development zones, tax incentives, inexpensive land, good weather, and new public-financed infrastructural connections for transportation of goods and services.

27—Ports of Los Angeles/Long Beach, California
The Port of Los Angeles is a Foreign Trade Zone (FTZ), established in 1994. It comprises about 2,700 acres of property, including warehousing facilities compatible with FTZ operations. The U.S. has over 230 FTZs in fifty states.

[21] Cohen and Zysman, *Manufacturing Matters*, 158. See also Michael J. Piore and Suzanne Berger, *Dualism and Discontinuity in Industrial Societies* (Cambridge: Harvard University Press, 1980).
[22] For a fascinating debate on Scott's theory of post-Fordism see the following: John Lovering, "Fordism's Unknown Successor: A Somment on Scott's Theory of Flexible Accumulation and the Re-emergence of Regional Economies," *International Journal of Urban and Regional Research* 14.1 (1990): 159–74; A. J. Scott, "Flexible Production Systems: Analytical Tasks and Theoretical Horizons–A Reply to Lovering," *International Journal of Urban and Regional Research* 15.1 (1991): 130–34; John Lovering, "Theorizing Postfordism: Why Contingency Matters (a further response to Scott)," *International Journal of Urban and Regional Research* 15.2 (1991): 298–301; A.J. Scott, "A Further Rejoinder to Lovering," *International Journal of Urban and Regional Research* 15.2 (1991): 302. For other uses of the term see Edward W. Soja, "The Postfordist Industrial Metropolis," *Postmetropolis* (Oxford: Blackwell, 2000), 156–88.
[23] "A salient feature of the new flexible ensembles of productive activity identified above is that…there was little to keep them attached locationally to the old centers of Fordist mass production. They had no special demand for the types of inputs and labor available in such centers, and they were at the outset relatively free to locate in a variety of geographical environments. Moreover, the old centers with their high levels of worker unionization and their relatively politicized working-class populations-leading to stubborn rigidities in both the workplace and the local labor market-constituted hostile milieu in several respects for the new flexible ensembles…As a consequence many, *but by no means all*, of the producers in the new ensembles began to seek out alternative kinds of locational environments uncontaminated by previous historical experience of large-scale manufacturing activity and Fordist employment relations." A. J. Scott, "Flexible Production Systems and Regional Development," *International Journal of Urban and Regional Research* 12.1 (1988): 178.
[24] A. J. Scott, "High-Technology Industrial Development in the San Fernando Valley and Ventura County: Observations of Economic Growth and the Evolution of Urban Form," *The City*, eds. Edward W. Soja and Allen J. Scott (Berkeley and Los Angeles: University of California Press, 1996), 276–310.
[25] Arizona Association for Economic Development.

Phoenix and other Sunbelt cities are ripe for attracting flexible industries because they offer special economic- and free trade–development zones, tax incentives, inexpensive land, publicly financed infrastructural connections for the transportation of goods and services, and in-migration of low-wage labor (see figures 26, 27).

Agglomeration and Regionalism
In planning and geography nomenclature, an "agglomeration" is defined as a built-up zone outside a traditional central city or town area. It is a distinct center or cluster of production, where industries and enterprises share various advantages of geographical proximity (such as ease of transporting goods, infrastructure costs, tax incentives, manufacturing-related product, and so on to act as an independent concentration of employment and economic production. Agglomeration typically occurs along the urban periphery, within close proximity of the leading edges of urbanization (see figures 28, 29). Newer peripheral agglomerations have a symbiotic, regional relationship to older central cities where industrial production formerly occurred, although they visually and physically appear as disparate urban forms and locations.
    One ardent supporter of economic regionalism is Michael Storper, professor at the London School of Economics and Political Science. Along with Scott, he believes regional-scale issues provide the key to understanding the metropolis as it shifts from Fordist to post-Fordist economies. While agreeing that agglomeration is increasingly becoming part of

28—Agglomeration along Interstate Highway 77, north of Charlotte, North Carolina
Charlotte's central county, Mecklenburg, contains more than 282 trucking companies and 600 transportation and warehousing companies, located along three major Interstate highways.

globalized production systems, Storper refutes overarching explanations for post-Fordism. Instead he argues for a more "site-specific" approach to understanding the economy of agglomeration by suggesting that new geographical proximities take advantage of flexible modes of production. Storper sees the resurgence of the region as the center of post-Fordist production because it is the least risky location in which to conduct economic activity. In *The Regional World*, Storper argues: "It became evident that even with increasing intensity of global trade and investment flows, national specificities in terms of products traced and technologies produced were increasing: in certain respects, integration was not bringing similarity, but specialization, a form of regionalization."[26]

Storper's thesis of regionalism is particularly interesting for designers because it suggests that new geographic space is created specifically for each agglomeration's most effective economic function, thus linking physical form to capital flow. Agglomerations and the customized infrastructures that support them produce unique types of places (such as industrial parks, intermodal hubs, Free Trade Zones, transportation corridors, and warehouse districts) in order to function in the most economically efficient manner. Subsequently an agglomeration's design may allow for new social interactions and information exchanges that support its viability.[27] While research is currently limited to support this supposition, Storper's "site specificity" raises important questions for designers. What do agglomerations look like? How do agglomerations function? How do people interact in agglomeration settings? How may designers understand and improve upon agglomeration environments?

In summary, as respective locations of economic (or industrial) production, the old central city and the new peripheral agglomeration share a regional relationship: they are active integrators of waste landscape. The former integrates waste landscape through the attrition of former industrial sites; the latter integrates waste landscape through the accumulation of new agglomerations.

Local and Regional Agglomerations
A reason for renewed interest in regionalism is social capital. Agglomerations require business partners, governments, and communities to work together at a regional scale to thrive. Advocates of regionalism believe that an appropriate balance of trust and frequent face-to-face contact takes place at the regional scale but not very effectively at larger international or global ones. It is therefore critical to understand how agglomeration design, at local and regional levels, may accommodate these social encounters.

Waste landscapes form as the result of agglomeration development at both local and regional scales. Locally, waste landscape forms inside of agglomerations (three to ten firms share one complex and circulation system). The landscape of a local (or site-specific) agglomeration is best described as low-rise, nondescript, tilt-up warehouses and paved surfaces.

29—Agglomeration at Fulton County Airport, Georgia, about twelve miles west of Atlanta
Although they visually and physically appear as disparate urban forms and locations, newer peripheral agglomerations have a symbiotic, regional relationship with older central cities where industrial production formerly occurred.

[26] Michael Storper, *The Regional World: Territorial Development in a Global Economy* (New York: The Guilford Press, 1997), 4, 9.
[27] Ibid., 9.

The local agglomeration is engineered for train and truck movement, and its associated warehouses and buildings are oriented internally to serve product circulation (see figures 30, 31). The landscape exists solely as the result of the agglomeration's needs: efficient manufacturing, packaging, staging, and inexpensive transportation of goods. Its landscape characteristics include flat topography (as a result of leveling), flat areas of turf grass or gravel (for ease of maintenance), lack of trees or overhead vegetative canopy (for security surveillance), and few to no human-scale amenities (except for smoker's pits or picnic tables for lunchgoers). The landscape is not designed to bring extraordinary value locally (such as unique ecological benefit or specially created animal or plant habitat). Instead it exists as a static, engineered component of the agglomeration's production economics.

Regionally, waste landscape forms outside of agglomerations, which develop at the peripheries of their respective central cities. Across a regional territory they tend to catalyze a reduction in land-use density and increased infrastructural costs due to the proliferation of single-family housing developments (for workers) and the use of the automobile as the primary mode of transportation. The widespread trend of locating manufacturing plants in areas outside city limits contributes to nonmetropolitan population growth and an abundance of waste landscape. Waste landscape accumulates everywhere: as buffer zones in between single agglomerations and their neighboring land uses, around the perimeters of housing enclaves, along new infrastructural right-of-ways, adjacent to roads and drainage ways, and within vast parking lots that surround office and retail complexes (see figure 32). Terrain that is too steep to accept leveling or inexpensive construction is bypassed by infrastructural improvements, thus becoming a waste landscape by default.

As agglomerations grow in number and size and regional economies expand, so does the opportunity for rethinking how their local and regional waste landscapes might in other ways be infilled with new agendas that create greater opportunities for face-to-face contact. As seen in Victor Turner's anthropological research (chapter 1), the waste landscapes spawned by local and regional agglomerations are liminal places where communitas may form. Conceived of in this manner, waste landscape benefits cities and regions and may result in designed or planned outcomes that serve the needs of the economy *and* those of the regional ecosystem and culture.

Technological Innovation and Location:
Waste Landscape and Space

Most directly, the Internet, express delivery systems, and related networks serve as key enablers of deconcentrating settlement and development patterns in North America.
–James Levitt, *Conservation in the Internet Age*

There is growing concern that decentralization and horizontal urbanization is linked to advances in telematics (communication technology). Those studying the effects of telecommunications on urban form assert that settlement patterns found in many North American cities and nonmetropolitan areas are facilitated by

30—Agglomeration along Interstate Highway 70, Denver, Colorado
Waste landscapes form as the result of agglomeration development at both local and regional scales. The landscape is not designed to bring extraordinary value locally or regionally (such as a unique ecological benefit or watershed function). Instead, it exists as a static, engineered component of the agglomeration's production economics. Downtown Denver is in the background.

31—Ground view detail within figure 30
The local agglomeration is engineered for train and truck movement, and its associated warehouses and buildings are oriented internally to serve product circulation. The landscape exists solely as the result of the agglomeration's needs: efficient manufacturing, packaging, staging, and inexpensive transportation of goods.

"the new capabilities of telecommunications and telematics for supporting dispersed economic activities away from traditional urban centers."[28] This sort of outlook has implications for both the older, traditional city center and the newer outlying and peripheral areas of metropolitan regions (see figures 33, 34). This outlook leads to questions regarding the landscapes' relationships to technology in urbanization. How are urban landscapes affected by technological innovations? Is there a relationship between waste landscape and telematics? How do designers and planners take these issues into account when working in an urbanized area? This chapter explores several ideas asserting that urban landscape formation is associated with but not necessarily caused by technological innovation.

There is a dearth of literature offering satisfactory answers to the issues of telecommunications and their environmental implications for cities.[29] Most designers and planners are unaware of the extent to which technological innovation plays in new modes of urban centralization and decentralization. Because designers and planners remain wedded to tangible and formal aspects of urban design, the intangible world of telematics and telecommunications is often overlooked as a contributor to horizontal urbanization and waste-landscape formation.[30] Change is implemented with such speed that designers and planners cannot keep pace armed with modernist modes of professional practice. When most designers and planners conceptualize the technological networks that assist urbanization, they tend to focus on the familiar mechanical, industrial age, physical systems that can be physically seen and kinesthetically experienced (such as roads, bridges, waterways, buildings, and other infrastructure).

In recent years optimistic and pessimistic predictions have been directed at cities undergoing technological advancement. David Harvey, for example, envisions a positive trickle-down effect for urban conditions resulting from technological innovation: "Each bundle of innovations has allowed a radical shift in the way that space is organized and therefore opened up radically new possibilities for the urban process. Breaking with the dependency upon relatively confined bioregions opened up totally new vistas of possibilities for urban growth."[31] Conservationists paint a starkly different picture of the Internet and other technological networks. They argue that technologies are the "key enablers" of decentralization.[32] Others predict that while technological innovations may speed up decentralization of older core areas as industry relocates, they will not lead to the demise of the old industrial city. Older city areas will instead be reshaped with technological upgrades, retrofits, and new uses for former industrial sites. As geographers Stephen Graham

32—Northeast corner of Interstate Highway 75 / President George Bush Turnpike, Richardson / Allen, Texas, Collin County
Regionally, waste landscape accumulates everywhere: as buffer zones in-between single agglomerations and their neighboring land uses, around the perimeters of housing enclaves, along new infrastructural right-of-ways, adjacent to roads and drainage ways, and within the vast parking lots that surround office and retail complexes.

[28] Graham and Marvin, *Telecommunications and the City*, 42; also see James Levitt, ed., *Conservation in the Internet Age* (Washington, DC: Island Press, 2002), 63–98.
[29] Graham and Marvin, *Telecommunications and the City*, 240–41.
[30] Ibid., 73.
[31] David Harvey, *Justice, Difference and Politics* (Oxford: Blackwell, 1996), 412.
[32] James N. Levitt, "Networks and Nature in the American Experience," *Conservation in the Internet Age* (Washington, DC: Island Press, 2002), 21. Many of the essays in this book also argue that new technologies help conservation causes through the use of GIS and other natural-resource mapping software.

and Marvin Simon state: "Rather than seeing the 'end' of the city, these processes create a complex new patchwork of different types of spaces—some real and others configured electronically."[33] Saskia Sassen, professor of sociology at the University of Chicago, argues that major decentralization processes will not occur in the wake of technological innovation. She asserts that even with technologies that allow for the mentality of geographical separation and globalization, cities currently hardwired for technological advances (i.e., already having hard and soft infrastructures) will be the first places to benefit from technological advances. She posits that older, traditional city centers will expand into regional territories as markets and social capital shift. The resultant city will be more fragmented, but the city core will *not* be vacated under these conditions.[34]

The disintegration of dense, coherent, and centrally managed infrastructures resulting from deindustrialization has become the key weapon for supporting the virtues of the Fordist city. Architectural historian Christine Boyer at Princeton University, in her largely formal critique entitled "Figured and Disfigured Cities," asserts that the figured city is well composed by design rules and patterns,

33—Housing near Parker, Colorado, about twenty-five miles southeast of Denver, Douglas County
Telematics and telecommunications contribute to horizontal urbanization and waste landscape formation.

[33] Graham and Marvin, *Telecommunications and the City*, 336.
[34] Saskia Sassen, *Global Networks* (New York: Routledge, 2002), 40; Also see Graham and Marvin, *Telecommunications and the City*, 100.
[35] Christine Boyer, "The Great Frame-Up: Fantastic Appearances in Contemporary Spatial Politics," *Spatial Practices*, eds. Helen Liggett and David Perry (London: Sage), 81–109.
[36] H.G. Wells, Anticipations of the Mechanical & Scientific Progress Upon Human Life and Thought (New York: Dover Publications, 1999).

in contrast with the disfigured city, which is characterized by invisible and abandoned segments excluded from network infrastructure: "Not only will [the disfigured city] lose the cross-subsidies inherent within Keynesian and monopolistic models of network management, but it is likely to fail to attract new private entrants to transport, energy, communications and water markets."[35] Despite the historical merits, arguments such as this seem hopelessly nostalgic and desperate in the face of economic restructuring and market-driven development practices. Even if portions of the city are bypassed by current network infrastructures, new modes may connect them in unpredictable ways in the future. H.G. Wells, in 1902, predicted that downtown industrial centers would not be left abandoned but instead become entertainment agglomerations.[36] Charlotte, Atlanta, Cleveland, Detroit, Houston, San Jose, Denver, and Phoenix have recently built sports stadia, casinos, shopping malls, and amusement parks in their old central districts, mostly on land formerly occupied by industry (see figures 35, 36).

Technological innovations have resulted in cheap and easy access to satellite and other mobile forms of communication and expansive Internet infrastructure, providing incentives for people and industry to relocate outside traditional city centers. Urban peripheries provide corporations with lower land costs, easy access, relaxed zoning codes, affordable housing, services, and newer amenities for their employees. Industries conduct business on the periphery while still linked to global markets. From 1979 to 1999 the location of office space and office employment in thirteen of the nation's largest metropolitan commercial real-estate markets shifted from traditional downtowns to outlying areas.[37] This movement reflects the strong trend toward developing residential lands outside older parts of the city. The same holds for manufacturing establishments and high-technology centers (see figures 37, 38).[38]

Recent literature regarding the effects of technology on urbanization smacks of anti- and pro-technology ideologies (depending upon a given author's position on urban sprawl and land conservation). However, there are two points upon which almost all agree: technological innovation alters our conception of location and space, and advances in telecommunication and transportation networks have afforded individuals and businesses locational flexibility.

Flows

The fixity of place (as opposed to locational flexibility) is radically challenged by technological innovations. Centrality is no longer a spatial phenomenon. In the early 1990s Manuel Castells, professor of sociology, city and regional planning, at the University of California at Berkeley, acknowledged the profound changes in our conceptions of location and space that result from proliferating technological innovations. Neither the organization nor their development process of recognizable, central, densely formed and populated cities is fixed any longer. Castells states:

34—Antennae farm near Concord, North Carolina
Technological innovation alters our conception of location and space, and advances in tele-communication and transportation networks have afforded individuals and businesses global locational flexibility.

[37] Lang, "*Office Sprawl*," see also Lang, *Edgeless Cities*.
[38] U.S. Census, U.S. Bureau of Labor Statistics.

While organizations are located in places, and their components are place-dependent, the organizational logic is placeless, being fundamentally dependent on the space of flows that characterizes information networks. But such flows are structured, not undetermined. They possess directionality, conferred both by the hierarchical logic of the organization as reflected in instructions given, and by the material characteristics of the information systems infrastructure…. The consequences of this conclusion are far-reaching, because the more organizations depend, ultimately, upon flows and networks, the less they are influenced by the social contexts associated with the places of their location.[39]

Castells's "space of flows" predicts major consequences for older city cores due largely to ensuing technological innovations. He analyzes the proliferation of new office developments, described as "nodal areas created by information-age, technology driven industry." Castells argues (as do others noted above) that automation technologies have allowed new office developments to decentralize and move to outlying areas. The resultant relocation has led to job losses in major central business districts. He concludes that information technologies and their new economies have led to massive suburban decentralization.[40] However dire this condition, Castells hopes that novel organizations, processes, and categories of urbanization may be found in this new space.

Arguments such as Castells's have been termed "technologically deterministic."[41] This school of thought tends to analyze and argue for cause and effect relationships between technology and urban conditions.[42] One of the more technologically deterministic writers of recent times, Joel Kotkin, believes that technology reshapes American landscapes in ways not seen since the onset of the Industrial Revolution: "Just as the railroad, telegraph, and mass-production factory produced the manufacturing cities and towns of the industrial economy, the rise of the digital economy is creating a new geography of economic life."[43] A central point in Kotkin's argument is that the high-technology economy has shifted jobs from the older city core toward peripheral areas because "new high-tech economy and sprawl are deeply intertwined."[44] He calls this phenomenon "outside-in," or the idea that the formation of work is coming from the outside of the old core areas, thus forming a new "digital geography." The digital geography, says Kotkin, has a workplace. It is shaped by technological innovations that create a more "elastic" locational choice for work.[45] Spatial fixity of work becomes less and less important as technology

35—Downtown Houston, Texas (opposite, top)
Two sports stadiums have been built in the downtown area since 1997: Minute Maid Park (formerly Astros Field, Enron Field, and the Ballpark at Union Station) and the Toyota Center. Both are home to professional sports franchises. Charlotte, Atlanta, Cleveland, Detroit, San Jose, Denver, and Phoenix recently built sports stadia, casinos, shopping malls, and amusement parks in their old, central core districts, mostly on land formerly occupied by industry.

36—Downtown Charlotte, North Carolina (opposite, bottom)
In the background is Bank of America Stadium (formerly Ericsson Stadium) opened in 1996, home of the NFL's Carolina Panthers. In the foreground is the new arena for the WNBA Charlotte Sting and the new NBA expansion team, the Charlotte Bobcats, who began play in 2004.

37—Research Triangle Park (RTP), Raleigh-Durham, North Carolina (above, top)
RTP lies within 7,000 acres of pine forest and has approximately 1,100 acres for development. It holds more than 100 research and development facilities which employ over 38,500 Triangle residents. The combined annual salaries in RTP amount to over $1.2 billion dollars.

38—University of Texas at Dallas and Texas A&M University Research and Extension Center, Plano, Texas (above, bottom)
Both schools sit within the LBJ Beltway (I-635) and Interstate Highway 75, or the "Telecom Corridor," which later became known as "Silicon Prairie" due to the high density of silicon chip manufacturing and research in the area.

[39] Manuel Castells, *The Informational City* (Oxford: Blackwell Publishers, 1999), 169–70.
[40] Ibid., 156–57.
[41] Graham and Marvin, *Telecommunications and the City*, 98; Daniel Bell, *The Coming of Post-Industrial Society* (New York: Basic Books, 1999), xxiv; Joel Kotkin and Fred Siegel, *Digital Geography: The Remaking of City and Countryside in the New Economy* (Indianapolis, IN: Hudson Institute, 2000), 12.
[42] Graham and Marvin, *Telecommunications and the City*, 80.
[43] Kotkin and Siegel, *Digital Geography*, 2–3.
[44] Ibid.
[45] Ibid., 7.

allows one to locate and conduct work anywhere that technology is available (see figure 39).

Despite their technologically determined perspectives, Castells's "space of flows," and Kotkin's "digital geography" move beyond entrenched formal critiques of urban spatial production toward an urbanism that is fluid and detached from physical space.[46] Rather than study urbanization through formalistic means such as graphic figure-ground configurations (pathetically unimaginative but still the most widely used reactive tool for urban-design analysis), one may now envision urbanization from discreet or combined points of view, including territorially, ecologically, economically, politically, and theoretically proactive ways. Urban theorist Sanford Kwinter describes this condition when he urges designers to "see the city as a volatile gas and no longer as an inert solid."[47] His reasoning is valuable because it shifts urbanization studies from being *reactive* to becoming *proactive*. In its largest sense, posits Kwinter, the study of urbanism is a massive set of interconnected distributed systems of production not permanently linked to a specific place.[48]

As communication replaces transportation as the primary mode of connection between people and the future costs of communication move significantly lower, the exodus from older parts of the city (where operating costs and personal expenses are higher and services lower) to newer outlying areas (where land is inexpensive and services are greater) will likely increase. Paraphrasing Daniel Bell's prediction in 1999 of an emerging "societal geography," one might say that spatial location no longer remains the controller of costs as communication systems save time and money. Distance becomes a function of time, not space.[49] Therefore, technological innovation intrinsically supports horizontal urbanization and must associate with the production of the waste landscapes therein.

Contamination, Ugliness, and Blight: Revaluing Waste Landscape

This is the landscape that nobody wants. It's my cup of rejection:
Driven to this unformed scraggly ignored backlot, this not-quite
Prairie, not-quite thicket, not even natural corner of
Texas, the hardscrabble left butt of a demoralized nation,
It is my choice and my pleasure to cherish this haphazard wilderness.
No, it's not even "wild." –it's a neglected product of artifice.
Come, let us walk by an improvised lakeshore, be given a vision:
Beaches of black dust, beautiful white ghosts, this drowned forest.
–Frederick Turner, *Texas Eclogues*

There are yet other types of waste landscapes. They accumulate throughout the American landscape as contaminated sites. Old airports, chemical and petroleum plants, landfills, intermodal hubs, and military installations are being decommissioned, closed, and redeveloped for new uses. As urbanization expands, these once isolated sites are now closer, and even abutting large populations. However, they cannot be

39—QVC Fulfillment Center (1.1 million square feet), along Interstate Highway 64, Edgecombe County, near Rocky Mount, North Carolina (above) Technological innovations have resulted in cheap and easy access to satellite and other mobile forms of communication and expansive Internet infrastructure, providing incentives for people and businesses to relocate outside traditional city centers.

[46]Sanford Kwinter, "Introduction: War in Peace," *Pandemonium* (New York: Princeton Architectural Press and Rice University School of Architecture, 1999).
[47]Ibid., 11.
[48]Ibid., 69; Sanford Kwinter and Daniela Fabricus, "The American City," *Mutations*, Rem Koolhaas et al., (Barcelona: Actar, 2000), 484.
[49]Bell, Coming of Post-Industrial Society, xlvii.

reused. They suffer from environmental degradation and pollution problems related to their former land uses, resulting in soil, groundwater, and building contamination (see figures 40, 41). The revaluing of contaminated, as well as ugly and blighted, sites (to be explained later in this section) is extremely relevant to contemporary issues of landscape and urbanization, in light of the previous discussion of deindustrialization and post-Fordism. In the past twenty years cities have become increasingly interested in reclaiming such places, returning them to productive use. This activity signals a paradigm shift for metropolitan and regional land-use-planning strategies, many of which consider sites containing environmental health risks a priority for redevelopment (rather than a liability).

There are three reasons for this shift in thinking. First, the federal government has developed new programs, policies, and funding mechanisms to promote reclamation and reuse of a wide range of contaminated sites. Second, local planning agencies have discovered that redeveloping contaminated sites can generate significant tax revenue. In response, policies and funding mechanisms to subsidize this activity are developed at the local level. Third, public attitudes regarding pollution and contamination have relaxed as the result

40—Landscape Contamination in the U.S. (below) In the past twenty years there has been a paradigm shift for metropolitan and regional planning agencies, who now consider sites containing environmental health risks a priority for redevelopment (rather than a liability). Many states have passed new legislation that make it easier and more lucrative for developers to build on "formerly" contaminated property.

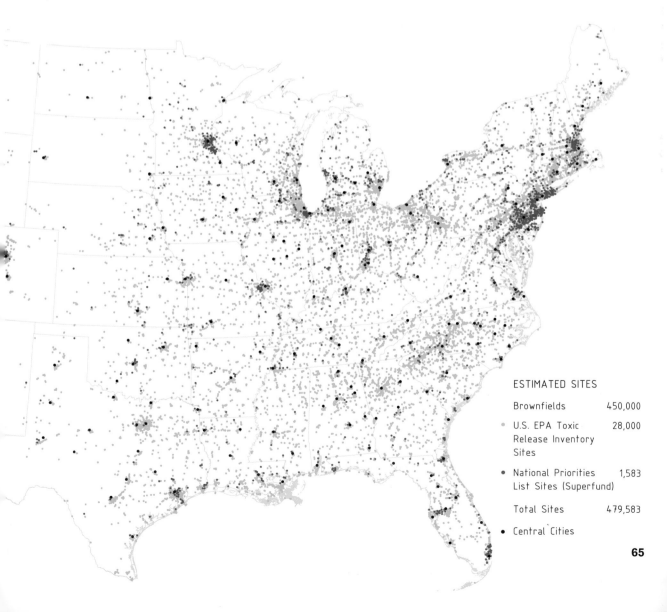

ESTIMATED SITES

Brownfields	450,000
U.S. EPA Toxic Release Inventory Sites	28,000
National Priorities List Sites (Superfund)	1,583
Total Sites	479,583
Central Cities	

of pro-development public-relations campaigns that have been supported by local governments. These entities seek quick-fix solutions for deficiencies in affordable urban housing and property-tax revenues in order to help pay for expanding infrastructure. These topics will be discussed within the context of redevelopment scenarios in American cities today.

Federal Activity
Between 1988 and 1995 the federal government closed ninety-seven major military bases around the country. Most had or still have some type of soil, water, or structural contamination that requires remediation. By 1998 the U.S. Department of Defense had completed thirty-five military-base property conveyances (transferring of the ownership title). By 1999, twenty-seven of these properties had undergone subsequent development.[50] Bergstrom Air Force Base, for example, in Austin, Texas, ceased operations in 1993. The site now contains the new Austin-Bergstrom International Airport and several office buildings. Land around the airport has dramatically increased in value. When Fort Devens in Ayer, Massachusetts, closed in 1996, the state purchased 3,040 acres from the federal government for $17.9 million. By 1999 the state had sold a hundred acres to developers, who turned the land into a million square feet of office, warehouse, and manufacturing space. The Gillette Corporation now occupies an $18 million warehouse

41—Houston Ship Channel, Texas
The San Jacinto Monument (upper right corner), located on the site where General Sam Houston's troops won independence for Texas in the 1800s, sits within one of the world's major refinery and petrochemical corridors. In 2001 and 2002 the average readings for vinyl chloride, a known human carcinogen, were recorded here as the most toxic in Texas. Each year more than 1.5 million tourists visit this site.

42—Fort Devens, Ayer, Massachusetts
Closed in 1996, the state purchased 3,040 acres from the federal government for $17.9 million. By 1999 the state had sold a hundred acres to developers who turned that land into 1 million square feet of office, warehouse, and manufacturing space.

[50] U.S. Department of Defense official web site, http://www.defenselink.mil/brac

and packing/distribution facility, as well as a $50 million manufacturing plant on the site (see figure 42). In Irvine, California, the nation's third largest home builder, Lennar, won an auction to buy the former El Toro Marine Corps Air Station for a record $650 million from the U.S. Department of Defense. El Toro redevelopment includes plans for 3,400 new homes in the heart of Orange County, California, the nation's hottest real-estate market (see figure 43). El Toro will be the largest of five major former military bases in California being redeveloped by Lennar. Other bases include 650 acres at Mare Island Naval Shipyard in Vallejo and more than a thousand acres in San Francisco's Hunter's Point Naval Shipyard and Treasure Island Naval Base.[51] The U.S. Department of Defense is continuing its evaluation of some 5,700 military installations for decommissioning or closure in the future (see figures 44, 45). A new round of military site closures was released by the U.S. Department of Defense in May 2005. It has already been determined or will be discovered that most of these sites contain some form of contamination. They will be transformed through private redevelopment into a variety of new civilian uses, which will take considerable time and investment.[52]

Denver: America's Superfund City

Perhaps better than any other rapidly urbanizing American region, Denver, Colorado, and the communities along the Rocky Mountain Front Range exemplify the new confluence of ecological attitudes and practices concerning contaminated land uses.[53] Sites along the Front Range urbanized area, totaling about 53,000 acres, are in the process of being converted from toxic land into redevelopment. The cleanup cost alone is estimated to be no less than $11 billion (see table 2 and figure 46).

Until recently the twenty-seven square-mile Rocky Mount Arsenal, now called the Rocky Mountain National Wildlife Refuge, was one of the largest urban toxic-land-reclamation projects in America. The Arsenal, a former chemical weapons, nerve gas and pesticide manufacturing site, was designated as a federal refuge in 1992.[55] Denver's most recently touted success story of toxic-urban-land conversion is the Rocky Flats Environmental Technology Site. Prior to 1989 it was a nuclear-trigger manufacturing plant, operated by the U.S. Department of Energy. Presently, it is undergoing a conversion process (like the Arsenal), which should transform it into a National Wildlife Refuge managed by the U.S. Fish and Wildlife Service.

After a raid by the FBI and the EPA, operations at Rocky Flats were shut down in 1989 in response to

43—El Toro Marine Corps Air Station, Irvine, California
In March 2005 the nation's third largest homebuilder, Lennar, won an auction to buy the former El Toro for a record $650 million from the U.S. Department of Defense. El Toro redevelopment will include 3,400 new homes in the heart of the nation's hottest real estate market, Orange County, California.

Table 2

Denver Metropolitan Area and Front Range Federal Superfund Sites

Superfund Sites	Size (acres)	Est. Cleanup Cost
Rocky Flats D	6,500	$ 7,743,362,832
Rocky Mountain Arsenal D	17,400	2,000,000,000
Pueblo Army Chemical Depot	22,654	1,200,000,000
Martin Marietta	160	80,331,034
Lowry Landfill D	480	63,000,000
Lowry Air Force Base D	1,866	57,600,000
Broderick Wood Products	64	27,276,752
Sand Creek Industrial D	350	29,832,097
Fitzsimmons Army Medical Center D	577	29,400,000
Denver Radium Sites D	n/a	26,363,455
Shattuck Chemical D	n/a	18,324,607
Woodbury Chemical	11	12,493,592
Chemical Sales	3,200	10,430,333
Marshall Landfill	160	2,991,776
Rulison/Rio Blanco	n/a	6,600,000
Stapleton Airport D	n/a	200,000
ASARCO Globe Plant D	89	n/a
Total[54]	**53,511**	**$11,308,206,478**

D = Denver metro area

[51] Jean O. Pasco, "One Bidder Wins It All at El Toro," *Los Angeles Times*, February 17, 2004.
[52] Dean E. Murphy, *New York Times*, "More Closings Ahead, Old Bases Wait for Hopes to Be Filled," May 15, 2005, Sunday, Section 1, Page 1, Column 4. Also see CNN's web site, "EPA: Closed military bases on list of worst toxic sites," http://www.cnn.com/2005/TECH/science/05/12/base.closings.environm.ap/index.html (accessed May 13, 2005).
[53] This title does not reflect empirical reality. The U.S. EPA lists Houston's Harris County as having the most National Priorities List (Superfund) sites. See a weeklong investigative report detailing the toxic-landscape problem in Houston's Harris County: *Houston Chronicle*, Monday January 17–21, 2005, http:// www.chron.com/toxics (accessed January 22, 2005).
[54] These numbers were compiled from the U.S. EPA's National Priorities List (Superfund) sites in Colorado, http://www.epa.gov/superfund/sites/npl/co.htm (accessed March 10, 2001).
[55] Berger, *Reclaiming the American West*, 31–32.

alleged violations of environmental statutes.[56] At one time Rocky Flats stored more than fourteen tons of plutonium. Building 771, the core facility for nuclear processing at the Flats, was even given the moniker of the "most dangerous building in America."[57] Groundwater beneath the site, on-site ponds, and lakes and reservoirs off-site were found to contain plutonium contamination. More than 2 million of the people in the eight-county Denver metropolitan area reside within a fifty-two-mile radius of the Rocky Flats site. More than three hundred thousand people live within ten miles of Rocky Flats. The closest residence to Rocky Flats is within two miles! Currently the site is surrounded by open space. Urban-growth pressures, however, are pushing residential and commercial development closer to the facility (see figure 47).

The final closure plans for Rocky Flats include landscape programs such as hiking and biking trails, nature-viewing areas, wetland and prairie habitat protection, a visitor's center, and active community-education programs. In a similar manner to the Arsenal's

44—Dobbins Air Reserve Base, Marietta, Georgia, about twenty miles northwest of Atlanta
Lockheed Martin Aeronautical Systems is building and testing the Air Force's F-22 advanced fighter, seen on a test run in this photo next to the smaller F-16 escort. Dobbins Air Reserve Base is the largest multi-service reserve training base in the world.

45—Seal Beach Naval Weapons Station, Seal Beach, California, about twenty-five miles southeast of Los Angeles
Seal Beach is the U.S. Navy's primary munitions storage and loading facility on the West Coast. The U.S. Department of Defense continues its evaluation of some 5,700 military installations for decommissioning and/or closure in the future.

[56] U.S. Environmental Protection Agency. Also see "Rocky Flats: Tread Warily, You Deer-Watchers–Turning Nuclear Sites into Wildlife Refuges Isn't That Easy," *The Economist*, February 24, 2005.
[57] "Energy Department to Begin Demolition of Rocky Flats Building 771, the Most Dangerous Building in America," U.S. Department of Energy, Office of Public Affairs, Washington, DC press release, July 14, 2004. This name is used extensively by the national media in response to descriptions of the building by the U.S. Department of Energy.
[58] See "Rocky Flats: Tread Warily, You Deer-Watchers–Turning Nuclear Sites into Wildlife Refuges Isn't That Easy," 32–33.
[59] KUSA-TV Denver, Colorado official web site, http://www.9News.com (accessed April 13, 25, 30, 2003).

education outreach program, Rocky Flats will receive busloads of school children and tourists each day to walk the area and learn about so-called "urban wildlife and ecology." A 2004 study by the Fish and Wildlife Service found traces of plutonium, americium, and uranium in two of twenty-six mule deer tested from the landscape buffer zone around the weapons-production area.[58]

Another interesting example of the new confluence of ecological attitudes and contaminated land use is Denver's Lowry Air Force Base. This site has seen many changes in occupation through the years. Lowry was a bombing range in the 1930s. It was converted into a landfill in the 1960s. In 1980 it was declared a Superfund site. Then, in the 1990s, it was redeveloped into several mixed-use neighborhoods and touted as a success story by the Congress for the New Urbanism. The 1,866-acre site is to be home to more than four thousand new residential units, a 156-acre college campus, an 86-acre business park, and almost 800 acres of parkland (see figures 48, 49). More than 1,500 dwelling units have already been built, with several hundred more under construction. In April 2003 ten vials discovered during home construction were feared to contain deadly mustard nerve agent. Fortunately they did not. Twelve days later construction was halted after asbestos was discovered in the soil. Subsequent tests revealed that eleven out of the hundred occupied Lowry homes contained asbestos-contaminated soils within their property. New home construction was halted until indoor air sampling proved the homes safe for occupancy.[59]

Contaminated plumes of groundwater running beneath the new development contain the toxic compound trichloroethylene (TCE), which was used in degreasers during aircraft-maintenance operations and was disposed of and stored in ways that affected the groundwater during the 1950s and 1960s.[60] Constant monitoring ensures that TCE does not become gaseous and enter homes through the soil under basements. Despite the alarming findings, which are regularly disseminated by public news outlets, residential development continues to attract new home buyers. Even after the asbestos issue was revealed, for example, Lowry's single-family-home appreciation outperformed most of Denver's market.[61] When the Congress for the New Urbanism and the City of Denver laud Lowry's success as a new urban community, there is little or no mention of its ongoing contamination problems.

Located within five miles of Lowry, Denver's former Stapleton International Airport is also being converted into a master-planned New Urbanist development.[62] The project opened a land mass one third the size of Manhattan (see figure 50). The former 4,700-acre airport is slated to comprise twelve thousand homes, 13 million square feet of commercial offices

46—ASARCO Globe Plant Superfund Site, Globeville, Colorado, three miles north of Denver
Since 1994 some 650 residential properties and seventy acres of commercial property had contaminated soil removed and replaced as part of the EPA's remediation plan.

47—Rocky Flats Environmental Technology Site, Jefferson County, Colorado, sixteen miles northwest of Denver
A former nuclear trigger manufacturing plant operated by the U.S. Department of Energy, which at one time stored more than fourteen tons of plutonium. More than 300,000 people live within ten miles of the site. The final closure plans for Rocky Flats include landscape programs such as hiking and biking trails, nature viewing areas, wetland and prairie habitat protection, a visitor's center, and active community education programs.

[60]Lowry Redevelopment Authority official web site, http://www.lowry.org/ecology/cleanup_sites.htm#asbestos (accessed June 14, 2005).
[61]Lowry Redevelopment Authority, Monthly Neighborhood Update, March 2004, 1.
[62]Forest City Stapleton, Inc. is the company overseeing redevelopment of the airport site, http://www.stapletondenver.com/main.asp (accessed June 14, 2005).

and retail space, 6 million square feet of office space, and 1,100 acres of parkland and open space. Construction of the first neighborhood and commercial area began in 2002. The site is expected to build out over a fifteen- to twenty-year timeframe. The old terminal parking structure and control tower are all that remain of the previous use. Stapleton's chemical de-icing methods contaminated the soil and groundwater in and around the airport. Nearly 700,000 cubic yards of contaminated soil have been treated or removed to toxic landfills. The subterranean plume of contaminated water will be monitored indefinitely. Developers and regulators claim that the site is "clean enough" for new home construction. Future toxic discoveries are likely, given the size and complexity of Stapleton's landscape, though this has not slowed development or buyer enthusiasm. The initial release of six hundred home units sold out in less than twenty-four hours.

Colorado, like many states, adopted new legislation that makes it easier and more lucrative for developers to build on "formerly" contaminated property. This followed Congressional passage of the 1997 Federal Taxpayer Relief Act (extended in 2000). This law included legislation to extend Brownfields tax incentives. These tax incentives include allowances for the costs of environmental cleanup to become fully deductible in the year they are incurred, rather than having to be capitalized. Other funding mechanisms of the law include revolving funds (loans), trust funds (tax or fee-based accounts), real estate investment trusts (REIT, or private investments), tax increment financing (TIF, described in detail below), tax incentives (credits and deferrals), and state grants.[63]

Brownfields

Since the 1990s brownfields have received increasing attention from the federal government. From 2003 to 2005 more than $225 million in federal grants were dispersed to states to promote the redevelopment of contaminated landscapes (see figure 51).[64] Most were former urban industrial-production sites. Today developers seek out contaminated sites instead of clean ones. A former director of the National Brownfield Association noted that developers can generate a higher rate of return from contaminated properties than from non-contaminated properties.[65] New federal subsidies for brownfield development make this possible. Tax increment financing, for example, allows for the taxes assessed on property value to be used for redevelopment activities such as infrastructure improvements.[66] One recent project is a

[63] Colorado Department of Public Health and Environment (CDPHE), http://www.cdphe.state.co.us/hm/bftaxhowto.asp (accessed June 14, 2005). Passage of the 2000 Colorado House Bill 00-1306 provided an additional income-tax credit for companies that redevelop contaminated property (Brownfields). For example, properties located in a municipality with a population of ten thousand or more persons may receive a maximum of $100,000 credit for cleaning each site. The bill also provides for limited state authority to clean up sites where there is no other federal or state program that can accomplish the cleanup. It provides $250,000 per site for such cleanup and redevelopment conditioning.
[64] U.S. EPA Brownfield official web site http://www.epa.gov/brownfields/archive/pilot_arch.htm (accessed May 21, 2005).
[65] Leon Hortense, "Squeezing Green out of Brownfield Development," *National Real Estate Investor*, June 1, 2003.

138-acre, 12 million square foot mixed-use complex on the site of a former Atlantic Steel Mill in midtown Atlanta. A developer paid $76 million to purchase the land in 1999. Even with $25 million in cleanup expenses, the total cost of the improved land was $732,000 per acre. A nearby uncontaminated site, purchased for the new home of the Atlanta Symphony, cost $22.3 million for 6.36 acres, or about $3.5 million per acre.[67] City leaders in Chicago, which currently has one of the nation's most aggressive brownfield redevelopment programs, agreed to sell a 573-acre former steel mill site along the shores of Lake Michigan to a team of developers for $85 million (see figure 52).[68] This site had produced steel for warships and skyscrapers for more than a century. It will be transformed into a mixed-use neighborhood for tens of thousands of residents.[69]

The term brownfield, however, is somewhat confusing and difficult for most people to comprehend. The majority of U.S. cities do not have a brownfield department or program. The reason for this is that the actual number of urban sites containing real (not perceived) contamination is unknown.[70] Cities typically apply for federal brownfield funding (described in the next section) in order to assess the levels of contamination on sites perceived to have such conditions (e.g., former industrial sites). Oftentimes no significant contamination is revealed, thus increasing the land's value and enabling rapid public or private redevelopment. When contamination is found, depending on its extent and severity, land value is significantly decreased, as the site must be cleaned of contaminants prior to redevelopment. Cities do not map brownfields! They do not want land value to decrease until there is substantiated evidence of contamination. Since there is insufficient federal funding to assess every urban site perceived to be contaminated, brownfield redevelopment will remain an ad hoc operation in the near future. Cities, therefore, will apply for federal assistance for brownfield assessment only when a party is interested in purchasing or redeveloping a given site (see figure 53).

Home Depot, a chain of home-improvement stores, actively seeks to develop store locations on urban brownfield sites. Home Depot's site-development strategy typically includes the excavation and relocation of toxic soil to the parts of the site planned for the store's vast parking lot. The building footprint is then laid down on the area of clean soil or on areas where toxins were removed or reduced below legal levels. This practice is obviously quite lucrative. Home Depot saves large sums of money on the purchase of land.

Contamination and abandonment may also bring favorable ecological surprises. Ecologists often find much more diverse ecological environments in brownfield sites than in the native landscapes that surround them.[71]

48, 49—Former Lowry Air Force Base Site, Denver, Colorado (opposite, top and middle) Touted as a success story by the Congress for the New Urbanism, this 1,866-acre site is to be home to over 4,000 new residential units, a 156-acre college campus, an 86-acre business park, and almost 800 acres of parkland. Top: Asbestos abatement of the soil prior to construction of a luxury townhouse. Middle: Soil tests revealed that 11 out of 100 suspected newly occupied Lowry homes had asbestos-contaminated soils within their property. Children's playground equipment and machinery were wrapped in plastic as a precaution.

50—Former Stapleton Airport Site, Denver, Colorado (opposite, bottom) The former 4,700-acre airport is to contain some 12,000 homes, 13 million square feet of commercial offices and retail space, 6 million square feet of offices, and 1,100 acres of parkland and open space. Stapleton's chemical de-icing methods contaminated the soil and groundwater in and around the airport. Nearly 700,000 cubic yards of contaminated soil have been treated or removed to toxic landfills. The subterranean plume of contaminated water will be monitored indefinitely.

[66] Brownfields Tax Incentive Fact Sheet, EPA Document Number: EPA 500-F-01-339, http:// www.epa.gov/brownfields/bftaxinc.htm (accessed June 17, 2005).
[67] Ibid.
[68] Southeast Chicago Development Commission official website, http://www.southeastchicago.org/html/enviro.html (accessed June 18, 2005).
[69] Lori Rotenberk, "Chicago Aims to Transform Site of Former Steel Mill," *Boston Globe*, May 21, 2004.
[70] Kirkwood, *Joint Center for Housing Studies.*
[71] Davis, *Dead Cities*, 385–86.

Brownfield Redevelopment Funding Budget (450,000 sites est.)

Brownfield Sites Awarded Funding

2004

$250 million

300

1993

$200 thousand US

1

Because of their contamination, industrial contexts, and secured perimeters, brownfield sites offer a viable platform from which to study urban ecology while performing reclamation techniques. These sites have the potential to accommodate new landscape design practices that concurrently clean up contamination during redevelopment, or more notably where reclamation becomes integral to the final design process and form.

Funding

Outside of Superfund and state, private, and nonprofit investment, the U.S. Environmental Protection Agency's brownfield program is the largest federal funding source solely available for cleaning up urban contaminated landscapes. Although the term brownfield has become commonplace, its lawful context paints a clearer picture of the intentions of the legislation. As referenced in a 2002 federal law (Small Business Liability Relief and Brownfields Revitalization Act) brownfields were not created solely for the sake of pollution removal. Their purpose was two-fold: 1–to reduce the exposure to liability resulting from the Comprehensive Environmental Response, Compensation, and Liability Act of 1980 (CERCLA) of persons wanting to redevelop contaminated land, and 2–to provide federal seed money to locate, assess, and clean up the contaminated land parcels. The law provides seed money for cleaning contaminated landscapes and, by reducing their liability, significant incentive to attract developers.

The brownfields program has several other funding mechanisms to encourage redevelopment. Brownfields tax incentives (part of the 1997 Federal Taxpayer Relief Act) allow developers to immediately reduce their taxable income by the cost of their eligible cleanup expenses.

51—Urban Landscape Contamination in the U.S.
The federal government estimates that tax incentives cost nearly $300 million annually in lost tax revenue. However, it expects to leverage more than $5 billion in Brownfields cleanup and redevelopment funding from the private and public sectors and return eight thousand sites to productive use.

52—Former U.S. Steel Plant Superfund Site, South Side Chicago, Illinois
Along the shores of Lake Michigan, Chicago city leaders agreed to sell a 573-acre former USX steel mill site to a team of developers for $85 million. The Sears Tower is in the background.

53—Beacon Park Yards, Allston (Boston), Suffolk County, Massachusetts
Beacon Park Yards has served as a rail transfer point since the Civil War. The current owner, CSX Corporation, inherited the cumulative chemical and fuel spillage from over a century of industrial use. Herbicides are intensively sprayed to keep the tracks and surface clear of obstructions. Many other toxic compounds have accumulated in the soil. New development encroaching this site potentially includes the reuse of Beacon Park Yards, which will require extensive and costly environmental cleanup.

This incentive creates an immediate tax advantage on these expenses, thus helping to offset short-term cleanup costs. To receive this tax incentive, the property earmarked for redevelopment must be located in a Census tract area where greater than 20 percent of the resident population is below the mean poverty level. In addition, among other requirements, the population must be less than two thousand and have 75 percent or more of the area's land zoned for industrial or commercial use. Many areas fitting this description are located within traditional city centers that experienced industrial and manufacturing job losses as a result of deindustrialization, post-Fordist modes of production, and technological networks that allow for location flexibility. The federal government estimates that tax incentives cost nearly $300 million annually in lost tax revenue. However, it expects to leverage more than $5 billion in brownfields cleanup and redevelopment funding from the private and public sectors and return eight thousand sites to productive use.[72] Developers reap the rewards of reusing inexpensive, urban, contaminated waste landscapes and enjoy limited liability and high resale value.[73] Municipalities similarly prosper from redevelopment of contaminated sites and the collection of tax revenues. In the end, cities may gain the most by finding new uses for waste landscapes that otherwise would be left vacant, abandoned, or, even worse, continue to sustain or produce contamination. The long-term costs and health risks associated with these reclaimed contaminated properties, however, are yet to be realized and measured.

Ugliness, Blight, and Tax Increment Financing
Cities, developers, and citizens are experiencing the renewed value of toxic, polluted, and contaminated lands. Redeveloping such properties creates urban territory for in-migration, employment, and construction. New financing mechanisms and legislation at federal and state levels make it easier than ever before to redevelop contaminated land with limited liability. This creates another interesting paradox concerning the redevelopment of urban land: the reuse of ugly or underproductive property. Cities characterize this type of property as blight. They ubiquitously use the funding mechanism, "tax increment financing" (TIF), for "blighted property" redevelopment. Blight and TIF are used hand in hand by city governments for redevelopment purposes.

TIF is a flexible funding incentive. Its original purpose was to offset the redevelopment costs of urban areas by enabling city governments to give tax breaks to developers and improve land values. Instead of paying property tax, for example, a developer could divert these taxes to pay for infrastructural improvements (sidewalks, roads, etc.) on a project site or to connect the site to an adjacent area. Some states allow TIF financing on brownfields. Others only allow it for blighted areas. Still others use it to lure new construction to outlying areas. A rapidly growing use of TIF financing is attracting "big box" retailers to urban areas that are experiencing economic decline. Under this scenario an urban-renewal authority (or city agency overseeing

[72] For a full variety of funding mechanisms available to help redevelop Brownfields see U.S. Environmental Protection Agency, http://www.epa.gov/brownfields/funding.
[73] U.S. Environmental Protection Agency.

such matters) attempts to declare eminent domain on a property as the result of blight, evict its tenants, give landowners a "fair market" price, and offer the site to a company along with substantial long-term tax breaks.[74]

In order to redevelop sites according to city planning interests, "blight" is preemptively used by city governments as a means to lawfully seek eminent-domain rights from individual property owners. Cities are increasingly designating property as "blight" not because it exhibits the aforementioned conditions such as toxicity, but because the city views the property as unproductive (from a tax-revenue perspective or an aesthetic one). Each city and local government opportunistically defines blight according to its own needs for redevelopment. There is no single definition for the actual composition of blight (see table 3).

Hundreds of abusive eminent-domain cases are reported as the result of this redevelopment strategy. Grass-roots organizations, civil-liberty coalitions, and activist groups, as well as litigation teams that specialize in individual property rights, have fought against such planning policy.[75] Nonetheless, cities continue to use the tools of blight and eminent domain to redevelop large urban areas, applying some of the same financing mechanisms that have been created to redevelop contaminated sites.

More so than at any other time during American urbanization, the current physical, financial, legislative, and legal systems are in place to rapidly redevelop the urban properties and adjoining ecological systems that were once designated as contaminated by toxins. Public acceptance of this land-development protocol is now widespread. Piggybacking on this protocol is the unfortunate redevelopment practice of blight designation as a means to remove "ugly and unproductive" property. To further complicate matters, in June 2005 the U.S. Supreme Court ruled that cities may legally seize private property for economic development even if that property is not blighted or contaminated. The ruling clears the way for any city to seize private land that it believes will receive a higher property-tax revenue with a new "public use," which will be defined by each state. Together, for better and worse, these funding mechanisms and policies greatly contribute to the creation and absorption of waste landscapes in American cities.

Table 3
Sampling of Blight Definitions

Frederick, Maryland
"Blighted Area" shall mean an area in which a majority of buildings have declined in productivity by reason of obsolescence, depreciation or other causes to an extent they no longer justify fundamental repairs and adequate maintenance.[76]

State of Virginia
"Blighted area" means any area within the borders of a development project area which impairs economic values and tax revenues, causes an increase in and spread of disease and crime, and is a menace to the health, safety, morals and welfare of the citizens of the Commonwealth; or any area which endangers the public health, safety and welfare because commercial, industrial and residential structures are subject to dilapidation, deterioration, obsolescence, inadequate ventilation, inadequate public utilities and violations of minimum health and safety standards; or any area adjacent to or in the immediate vicinity thereof which may be improved or enhanced in value by the placement of a proposed highway construction project.[77]

Carson City, California
"Blighted area" is an unproductive condition of land; loss of population. A blighted area is characterized by: a) in some parts of the blighted area, a growing or total lack or proper utilization of areas, resulting in a stagnant and unproductive condition of land potentially useful and valuable for contributing to the public health, safety, and welfare; b) in other parts of the blighted area, a loss of population and reduction of proper utilization of the area, resulting in its further deterioration and added costs to the taxpayer for the creation of new public facilities and services elsewhere.[78]

Cleveland, Ohio
"Blighted premises" shall mean premises which because of their age, obsolescence, dilapidation, deterioration, lack of maintenance or repair or occurrence of drug offenses, prostitution, gambling and other criminal acts which constitute public nuisances at the premises or any combination thereof, including the ineffectiveness of House Code enforcement after lawfully issued citations or violation notices, constitute an apparent fire hazard, place of retreat for immoral and criminal purposes constituting a public nuisance or repeated and serious breaches of the peace, health hazard, public safety hazard or any combination thereof; an unreasonable interference with the reasonable and lawful use and enjoyment of other premises within the neighborhood; or a factor seriously depreciating property values in the neighborhood.[79]

State of California Code
A "blighted area" is one that is predominantly urbanized, and is an area in which the combination of conditions [described in other codes] is so prevalent and so substantial that it causes a reduction of, or lack of, proper utilization of the area to such an extent that it constitutes a serious physical and economic burden on the community which cannot reasonably be expected to be reversed or alleviated by private enterprise or governmental action, or both, without redevelopment. A blighted area also may be one that is characterized by the existence of inadequate public improvements, parking facilities, or utilities.[80]

[74] One such example occurred in Denver, Colorado. The Denver Urban Renewal Authority wanted to grant Wal-Mart $10 million in tax subsidies to redevelop the Alameda Center, which had the largest Asian grocery food store in the city and arguably some of the best Asian restaurants. After a lengthy and raucous petition process, Wal-Mart backed out of its plans.
[75] Richard A. Epstein, *Takings: Private Property and the Power of Eminent Domain* (Cambridge: Harvard University Press, 1989). And Jerold S. Kayden, "Is Eminent Domain for Economic Development Constitutional?" *Harvard Design Magazine*, 22, Spring/Summer 2005, 67-70.
[76] City of Frederick, Maryland: under Appendix I–Urban Renewal Authory For Slum Clearance. Definitions, Sec. A1-101.
[77] Virginia General Assembly, Code of Virginia Chapter 32–Real Property Tax–Article 1–Taxable Real Estate § 58.1-3245. Definitions.
[78] Carson City, California-Community Redevelopment Law in 1974, State Policy Blighted Areas § 33030, Article 3, § 33034.
[79] Cleveland, Ohio, Title V–Community Development Code, Chapter 324, Section 324.03.
[80] State of California, Definition of Blighted Area Contained in California Health and Safety Code, Section 33030-33039.

Part Two
Representing the Relationships between Waste Landscape and Urbanization

Chapter Three
Ten Urbanized Regions

Measuring the dynamics of urbanization in order to see its effects on the landscape is a representational issue. This chapter presents the quantitative and visual analyses of ten major urbanized regions spread across diverse geographical locations of the U.S.–north to south, east to west. Waste landscapes (as defined in part one of this book) in each of the ten urbanized areas are composited using graphic representations that combine geospatial data, U.S. Census empirical findings, and spatial imagery (see Appendix Two: Notes on Graphics: Data Uses, Sources and Methods for a detailed explanation of the data compilations). These representations reveal how landscape and urbanization yield opportunities for reconceptualizing waste landscape in the urban world.

Entropic indicator maps simultaneously show the rapid spatial growth of urbanization from 1990 to 2000, and other specific large land area activities that have changed over this period. Large land area activities include uses such as golf courses, parks, military installations, airports, landfills, retail centers, housing, intermodal hubs, highways, and water bodies. U.S. EPA Toxic Release Inventory sites are also located in these maps to demonstrate where industry (see manufacturing sites on maps) has clustered in the past and where concentrations of soil and/or water contamination likely can be found. These activities constitute large landscape-dependent uses that have experienced a value transfer, or the production of entropy (such as disinvestment, consolidation, vacancy, etc.). Entropic production, according to the branch of physics known as nonequilibrium thermodynamics, leads to situations of increased complexity (Ilya Prigogine's *The End of Certainty*). Complexity is not achievable within an equilibrium state, in which all activity must be accounted for and balanced through imposed order (such as strict zoning codes and univalent masterplanning). By mapping locations of entropic production, such as landscape-dependent activities that have systematically changed over time through the processes described earlier in this book, one obtains an understanding of each region's waste landscape geography.

The entropic indicator maps function intertextually with two other unique sets of graphical analysis: dispersal graphs and spindle charts. The dispersal graphs exhibit peaks and dips where population density is high and low respectively. The dips run varying widths (measured in miles) to reveal the "in-between" and "external-frontier" landscapes. If one correlates population density and distance from the city center found on the dispersal graphs with areas of manufacturing activity found on the spindle charts and the land-use clusters found on the entropic indicator maps, the result is new, previously unforeseen spatial concentrations of a variety of waste landscapes from which future regional landscapes may be reclaimed for cultural and ecological benefits.

Atlanta

Boston-Lowell/
Providence

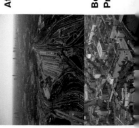

For example, one can conclude from the cities researched in this book that manufacturing establishments are progressively relocating forty to seventy miles outside of their traditional central city locations.

Likewise, information (plan/section, empirical/visual, fixed/temporary, etc.) may be read simultaneously and in multiple views and scales. Representational techniques provide the glue that enables the reader to cross-reference and derive new associations among disparate facets of urbanization over time. They add a time dimension. For example, spindle charts investigate both manufacturing decline and growth, enabling one to discern relationships between the old, contaminated, and technological obsolete and its opposite—the green, clean, and technologically connected.

Preconceived values (such as the fact that centrally located architectural density is more populated than peripheral housing areas) are also considered in the representations. Centrally located industrial zones, for instance, can be simultaneously compared with peripherally positioned residential areas. The Drosscape concept looks at all of the waste landscapes within urbanization: from wasted contaminated lands (usually located within central cities, and leftover from previous periods of industrialization), to wasteful sites of low density, horizontal development. The classic Drosscape signature exhibits the majority of wasted deindustrialized land near the city center, and the wasteful low density land around the city's periphery. As a result, Drosscape considers waste landscape from both old and new urbanization, and central and peripheral urbanization, without discrimination. All of these photographs were researched after the maps were delineated in order to locate and capture the specific geographic locational evidence revealed in the map within which it is nested. Photographs are nested and embedded in all of the graphics to provide site-specific evidence of the ground conditions revealed in the mapped or charted data. Waste landscapes can thus be observed simultaneously, from the scale of individual sites to entire urbanized regions.

Raleigh-Durham

Chicago

Cleveland/Akron

Dallas/Fort Worth

Denver/Front Range

Houston

Los Angeles

Phoenix

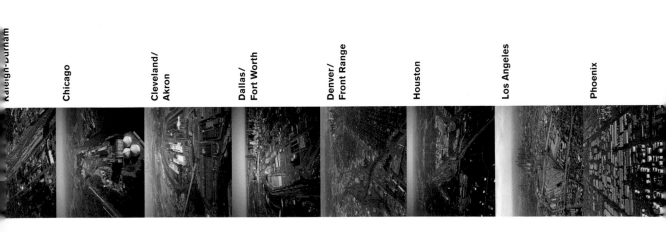

Atlanta

54—Norfolk Southern's Inman Yard/CSX's Tilford Yard, Fulton County, Georgia

More than 80 percent of the U.S. population lives within one day's interstate travel from Atlanta. This condition spawns a massive goods transportation network including these inner city railyards. Real estate speculation has begun in areas abutting these railyards because they are the largest tracts of undeveloped land inside of Interstate Highway 285.

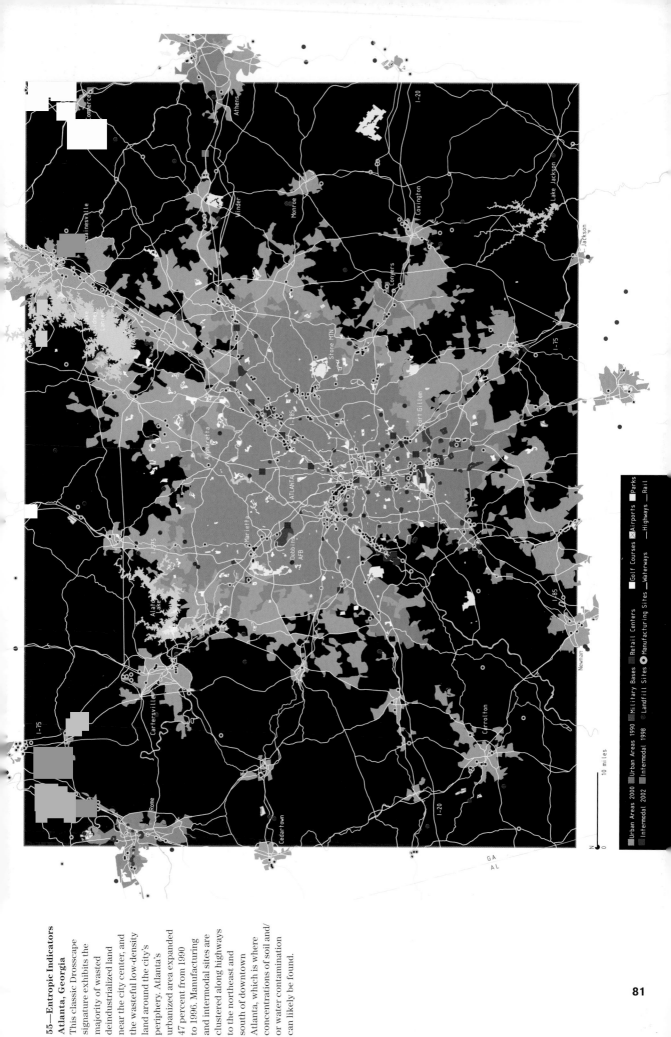

55—Entropic Indicators
Atlanta, Georgia
This classic Drosscape signature exhibits the majority of wasted deindustrialized land near the city center, and the wasteful low-density land around the city's periphery. Atlanta's urbanized area expanded 47 percent from 1990 to 1996. Manufacturing and intermodal sites are clustered along highways to the northeast and south of downtown Atlanta, which is where concentrations of soil and/or water contamination can likely be found.

Urban Areas 2000 Urban Areas 1990 Military Bases Retail Centers Golf Courses Airports Parks
Intermodal 2002 Intermodal 1998 Landfill Sites Manufacturing Sites Waterways Highways Rail

10 miles
N
0

81

56—Housing, Norcross area, Gwinnett County, Georgia

From 1990 to 2000 Gwinnett was the seventeenth fastest growing U.S. county adding 235,538 residents.

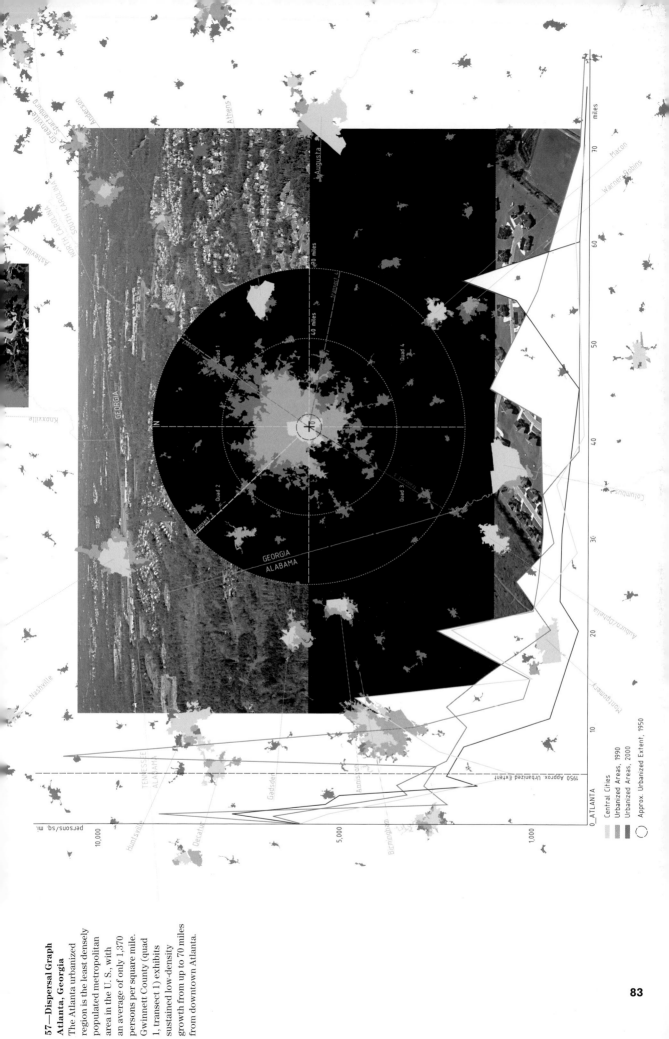

57—Dispersal Graph
Atlanta, Georgia
The Atlanta urbanized region is the least densely populated metropolitan area in the U. S., with an average of only 1,370 persons per square mile. Gwinnett County (quad 1, transect 1) exhibits sustained low-density growth from up to 70 miles from downtown Atlanta.

persons/sq. mi.

10,000

5,000

1,000

Central Cities
Urbanized Areas, 1990
Urbanized Areas, 2000
Approx. Urbanized Extent, 1950

0_ATLANTA

1950 Approx. Urbanized Extent

10   20   30   40   50   60   70

miles

58—Dekalb-Peachtree Airport and Gwinnett County Agglomeration, Georgia

Dekalb-Peachtree airport, located in the background, is the second busiest airport in Georgia in number of flights. It occupies the site of the former training base Camp Gordon, twelve miles northeast of downtown Atlanta. The agglomeration in the foreground is located in Gwinnett County. Kimberly Clark and Bank of America operate flight departments on the airfield.

**59—Spindle Chart
Atlanta, Georgia**

Since 1977 Fulton County, Atlanta's central county, lost 26 percent of its manufacturing establishments, while Forsyth County, located thirty-five miles outside of the central city, grew 431 percent during the same time.

■ Manufacturing Establishments Change, 1977–1992
■ Manufacturing Establishments Growth, 1992–2001
■ Manufacturing Establishments Decline, 1992–2001

COUNTY RANKING:
1977–2001

	% Change in Manufacturing Est.	Distance from Center (mi.)
HALL	64%	51.2
PICKENS	60%	48.3
NEWTON	135%	42.4
BARTOW	39%	40.8
SPALDING	22%	36.3
FORSYTH	431%	34.9
CHEROKEE	162%	31.1
HENRY	109%	26.9
GWINNETT	265%	26.2
COWETA	56%	34.8
ROCKDALE	106%	24.5
FAYETTE	167%	21.8
DOUGLAS	154%	20.5
CLAYTON	19%	16.2
COBB	111%	14.5
DEKALB	-7%	11.3
FULTON	-26%	0

New Peripheral Sites

(Gwinnett County)

Old Central Sites

(Fulton County)

85

Boston-Lowell / Providence

60—Downtown Lowell, Middlesex County, Massachusetts

Lowell's textile mills played a central role in the U.S. Industrial Revolution. These abandoned mills are located along the Merrimack River. The locks, canals, and facilities were transformed from cutting-edge manufacturing centers to derelict waste to highly valued components of a National Historic Monument in less than a hundred years.

**61—Entropic Indicators
Boston-Lowell,
Massachusetts /
Providence,
Rhode Island**

This classic Drosscape
signature exhibits the
majority of wasted
deindustrialized land
near the city center
and the wasteful low-
density land around the
city's periphery.

ATLANTIC OCEAN

Provincetown, MA

Cape Cod

Barnstable Town, MA

Camp
Edwards
AFB

New Bedford, MA

I-495

Cape Ann

Gloucester

I-95

I-495

I-95

BOSTON, MA

Manchester, NH

Nashua, NH

I-93

NH
MA

Fort
Devens
AFB

Lowell

PROVIDENCE, RI

MA
RI

Worcester

Keene

Leominster

MA
CT

Athol

Quabbin
Reservoir

I-90

Springfield

Urban Areas 2000 Urban Areas 1990 Retail Centers Golf Courses Airports Parks
Intermodal 2002 Intermodal 1998 Military Bases Landfill Sites Manufacturing Sites Waterways Highways Rail

10 miles

N

62—Littleton (between Boston and Lowell), Middlesex County, Massachusetts

During the 1990s Littleton morphed from a New England agricultural town into a bedroom community. The Interstate Highway 495 corridor grew 11.3 percent in the last decade, or twice as fast as the Greater Boston Region.

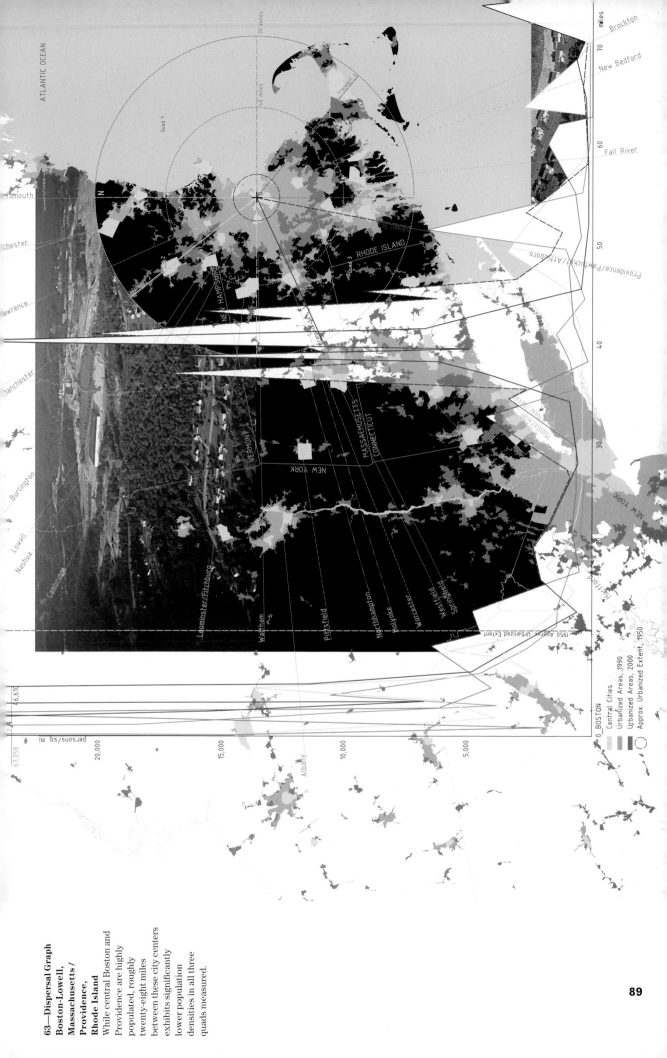

**63—Dispersal Graph
Boston-Lowell,
Massachusetts /
Providence,
Rhode Island**

While central Boston and
Providence are highly
populated, roughly
twenty-eight miles
between these city centers
exhibits significantly
lower population
densities in all three
quads measured.

ATLANTIC OCEAN

Quad 1

Quad 2

Quad 3   RHODE ISLAND

NEW HAMPSHIRE

VERMONT

NEW YORK

MASSACHUSETTS
CONNECTICUT

NEW YORK

Portsmouth

Winchester

Lawrence

Manchester

Burlington

Lowell

Nashua

Cambridge

Leominster/Fitchburg

Waltham

Pittsfield

Northampton

Holyoke

Worcester

Westfield

Springfield

Albany

Hartford

Middletown/New Britain

Providence/Pawtucket/Attleboro

Brockton

New Bedford

Fall River

40 miles

70 miles

N

0

1950 Approx. Urbanized Extent

67,058   persons/sq. mi.

46,610

20,000

15,000

10,000

5,000

0_BOSTON
    Central Cities
    Urbanized Areas, 1990
    Urbanized Areas, 2000
    Approx. Urbanized Extent, 1950

miles

70

60

50

40

30

20

10

89

64—Lumber Yard (between I-495 and Lowell), Middlesex County, Massachusetts The Interstate Highway 495 corridor rose by a staggering 62 percent, or 30,000 new jobs, in the service sector from 1990 to 2000. Manufacturing continues to decline throughout the Greater Boston Region.

65—Spindle Chart
Boston-Lowell,
Massachusetts /
Providence,
Rhode Island

Since 1977 the central counties in Boston and Providence have lost 61 percent and 49 percent of their manufacturing establishments, respectively. This region's greatest manufacturing growth is located in New Hampshire and Rhode Island, some forty-five to seventy miles outside of the central cities.

- Manufacturing Establishments Change, 1977–1992
- Manufacturing Establishments Growth, 1992–2001
- Manufacturing Establishments Decline, 1992–2001

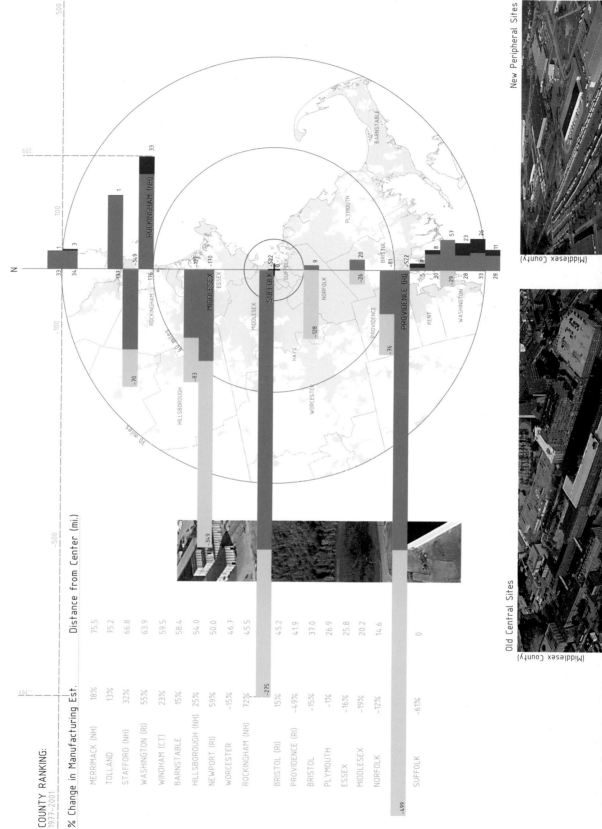

COUNTY RANKING:
1977–2001

	% Change in Manufacturing Est.	Distance from Center (mi.)
MERRIMACK (NH)	18%	75.5
TOLLAND	13%	75.2
STAFFORD (NH)	32%	66.8
WASHINGTON (RI)	55%	63.9
WINDHAM (CT)	23%	59.5
BARNSTABLE	15%	58.4
HILLSBOROUGH (NH)	25%	54.0
NEWPORT (RI)	59%	50.0
WORCESTER	-15%	46.7
ROCKINGHAM (NH)	72%	45.5
BRISTOL (RI)	15%	45.2
PROVIDENCE (RI)	-49%	41.9
BRISTOL	-15%	37.0
PLYMOUTH	-1%	26.9
ESSEX	-16%	25.8
MIDDLESEX	-19%	20.2
NORFOLK	-12%	14.6
SUFFOLK	-61%	0

Old Central Sites
(Middlesex County)

New Peripheral Sites
(Middlesex County)

Charlotte/
Raleigh-Durham

**66—Norfolk Southern
Freight Yard and Amtrak
Station, Mecklenburg
County, Charlotte,
North Carolina**

Rapidly urbanizing areas
such as Charlotte place
operational strain on older
infrastructures such as
this combined freight yard
and passenger station
from 1968, located two
miles northeast of
downtown. Charlotte
is strategically located
between Norfolk
Southern's and CSX's
extensive eastern U.S.
rail network. This
makes Charlotte a
critical transfer point for
products being shipped.
Land surrounding the
rail activities is in great
demand by the rail
companies for expanding
operations and those
who value proximity
to downtown.

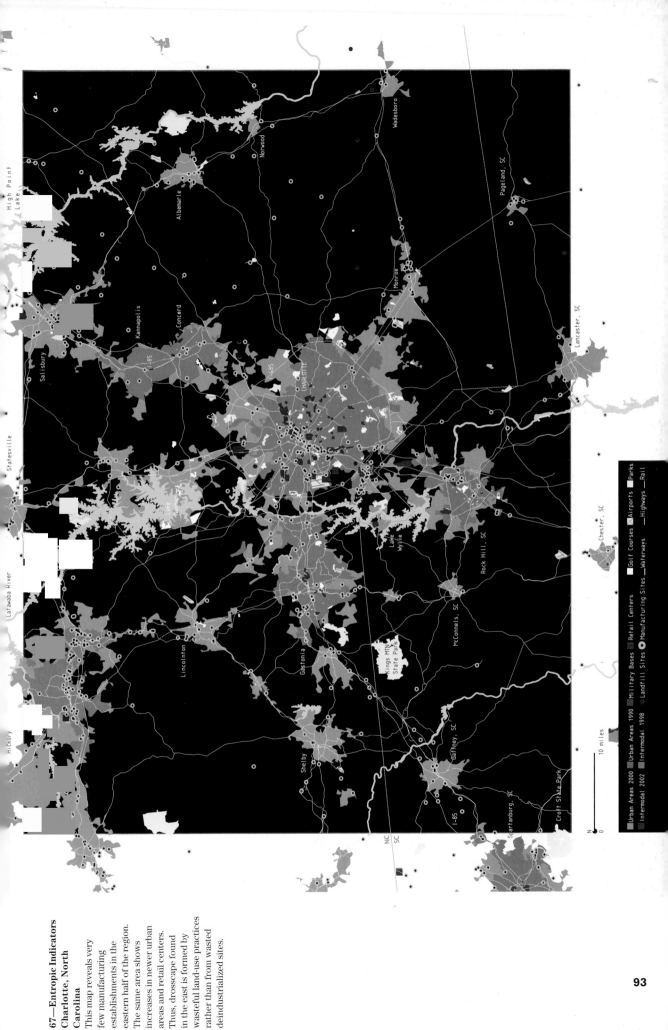

**67—Entropic Indicators
Charlotte, North
Carolina**

This map reveals very
few manufacturing
establishments in the
eastern half of the region.
The same area shows
increases in newer urban
areas and retail centers.
Thus, drosscape found
in the east is formed by
wasteful land-use practices
rather than from wasted
deindustrialized sites.

Urban Areas 2000 ■ Urban Areas 1990 ■ Military Bases ■ Retail Centers ■ Golf Courses ✕ Airports ■ Parks
Intermodal 2002 ⊛ Intermodal 1998 ⊛ Landfill Sites ⊙ Manufacturing Sites —Highways —Rail
—Waterways

N
0   10 miles

68—Housing (northeast of Raleigh) near Johnston County, North Carolina

Five counties in North Carolina are ranked in the top hundred fastest growing U.S. counties from 2000 to 2003. No. 95, Johnston County, grew by 14,878 people (a 12.2 percent increase) as Wake County workers migrated to reside there. North Carolina landscape is being developed at a rate of over 100,000 acres per year.

**69—Dispersal Graph
Charlotte, North
Carolina**
Population density
declines sharply within
a ten-mile radius from
the city center in all four
quads measured.

Central Cities
Urbanized Areas, 1990
Urbanized Areas, 2000
No Data, 1950

70—Former Cannon Mills factory in Kannapolis, Cabarrus/Rowan Counties, North Carolina

When Pillowtex Corporation (formerly Cannon Mills, the towel manufacturer) closed in 2003, 4,300 jobs were lost. More than 3 million jobs in the U.S. were lost as the result of economic restructuring from 2000 to 2004.

**71—Spindle Chart
Charlotte, North
Carolina**

Because of this area's
low density and proximity
to Atlanta, manufacturing
gains and losses are
not centralized. Stanly
County, thirty-four miles
from central Charlotte,
posted the region's
biggest manufacturing
establishment gain
of 180 percent.

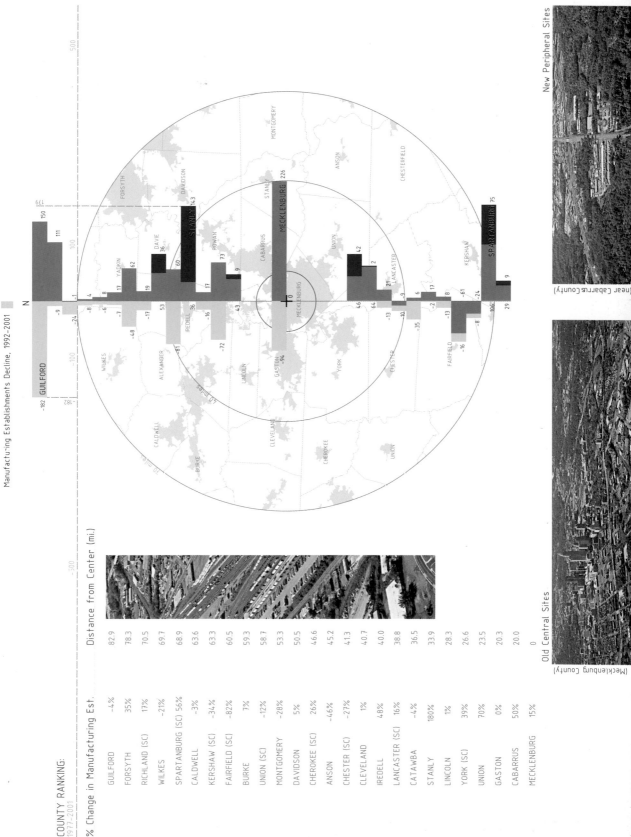

Manufacturing Establishments Change, 1977–1992
Manufacturing Establishments Growth, 1992–2001
Manufacturing Establishments Decline, 1992–2001

COUNTY RANKING:
1977–2001

% Change in Manufacturing Est.		Distance from Center (mi.)
GUILFORD	-4%	82.9
FORSYTH	35%	78.3
RICHLAND (SC)	17%	70.5
WILKES	-21%	69.7
SPARTANBURG (SC)	56%	68.9
CALDWELL	-3%	63.6
KERSHAW (SC)	-34%	63.3
FAIRFIELD (SC)	-82%	60.5
BURKE	7%	59.3
UNION (SC)	-12%	58.7
MONTGOMERY	-28%	53.3
DAVIDSON	5%	50.5
CHEROKEE (SC)	26%	46.6
ANSON	-46%	45.2
CHESTER (SC)	-27%	41.3
CLEVELAND	1%	40.7
IREDELL	4.8%	40.0
LANCASTER (SC)	16%	38.8
CATAWBA	-4%	36.5
STANLY	180%	33.9
LINCOLN	1%	28.3
YORK (SC)	39%	26.6
UNION	70%	23.5
GASTON	0%	20.3
CABARRUS	50%	20.0
MECKLENBURG	15%	0

Old Central Sites
(Mecklenburg County)

New Peripheral Sites
(near Cabarrus County)

Chicago

72—Calumet River Region, Cook County, Illinois

The Lake Calumet area has a cluster of Superfund sites including those used by U.S. Drum, Auburn Incinerator, and Paxton Lagoons (left of rail corridor). This area formerly contained two-hundred acres of wetlands around Calumet Lake, which was reduced by half its area through waste landfilling. The Southside Chicago area contains 60 percent of the region's vacant industrial property. Chicago is in the background.

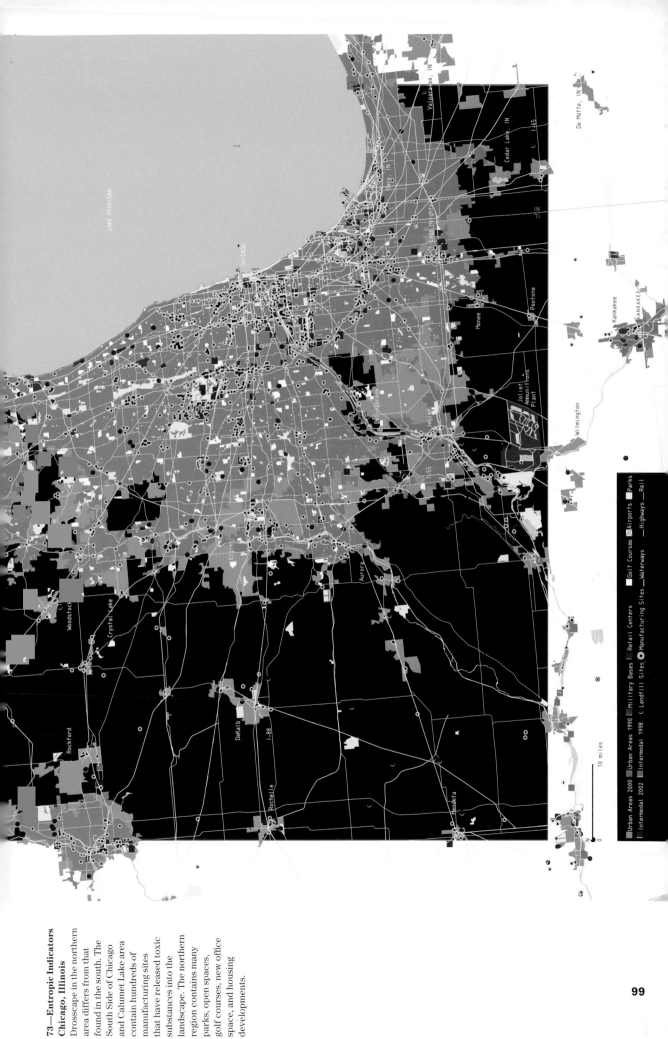

**73—Entropic Indicators
Chicago, Illinois**
Drosscape in the northern
area differs from that
found in the south. The
South Side of Chicago
and Calumet Lake area
contain hundreds of
manufacturing sites
that have released toxic
substances into the
landscape. The northern
region contains many
parks, open spaces,
golf courses, new office
space, and housing
developments.

Urban Areas 2000 ■ Urban Areas 1990 ■ Military Bases ■ Retail Centers □ Golf Courses ✕ Airports ■ Parks
| Intermodal 2002 ■ Intermodal 1998 〈 Landfill Sites ● Manufacturing Sites — Highways — Waterways — Rail

10 miles

74—Northeast of Joliet, the area along I-80 corridor, Will County, Chicago, Illinois
Will County is the fastest growing in the six-county region (13 percent from 2000 to 2003). The newest population growth and residential development is concentrated along the Interstate Highway 80 corridor between Joliet and the Interstate Highway 57 intersection.

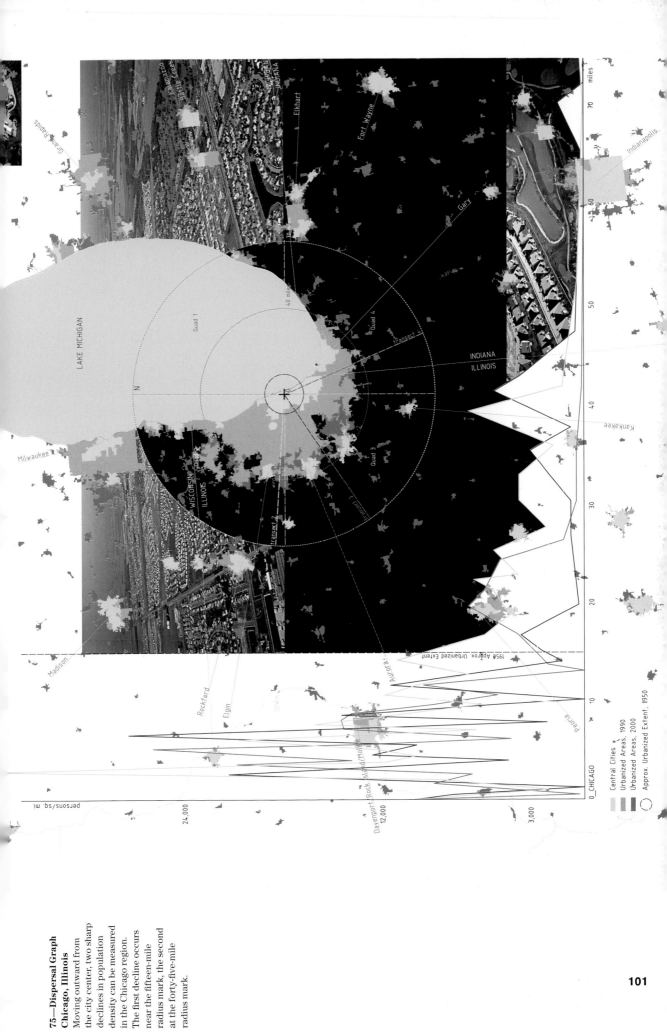

**75—Dispersal Graph
Chicago, Illinois**
Moving outward from
the city center, two sharp
declines in population
density can be measured
in the Chicago region.
The first decline occurs
near the fifteen-mile
radius mark, the second
at the forty-five-mile
radius mark.

**76—Speculative
warehouses and
agglomeration along
I-55, Bolingbrook/
Romeoville, Dupage
County, Illinois**

Real estate speculation
in this region takes the
form of business parks,
warehouse distribution
centers, and storage
facilities. New warehouses
agglomerate along the
Interstate Highway 55
corridor in anticipation
of population growth,
rising land values, and
new demand for goods.

Change in Manufacturing Establishments + Distance from Center

Manufacturing Establishments Change, 1977–1992
Manufacturing Establishments Growth, 1992–2001
Manufacturing Establishments Decline, 1992–2001

77—Spindle Chart
Chicago, Illinois

Since 1977, Cook County, Chicago's central county, has lost over four thousand manufacturing establishments, or a decline of 35 percent. The largest sustained manufacturing gains in this region are located thirty to fifty miles outside of the city center.

COUNTY RANKING:
1977–2001

% Change in Manufacturing Est.	Distance from Center (mi.)
OGLE	1%	87.4
WALWORTH (WI)	34%	71.2
BOONE	43%	68.5
NEWTON (IN)	4%	64.5
RACINE (WI)	-10%	63.9
DEKALB	30%	58.3
GRUNDY	-12%	57.0
KANKAKEE	10%	52.3
MCHENRY	69%	52.3
KENOSHA (WI)	50%	51.1
KENDALL	43%	45.4
		45.2
KANE	46%	41.3
PORTER (IN)	74%	40.9
LAKE	52%	36.7
WILL	66%	34.3
LAKE (IN)	1%	33.0
DUPAGE	50%	23.5
COOK	-35%	0

Old Central Sites
(Cook County)

New Peripheral Sites
(DuPage/Will County)

103

Cleveland/ Akron

78—Cuyahoga River Valley industrial area, Cuyahoga County, Cleveland, Ohio

Steel mills, gravel pits and the first oil refinery in the U.S. have all occupied this industrial area along the Cuyahoga River Valley. Cleveland's location between New York and Chicago make it ideal for industrial manufacturing and transportation using railroad infrastructure. The Aluminum Company of America is in the foreground.

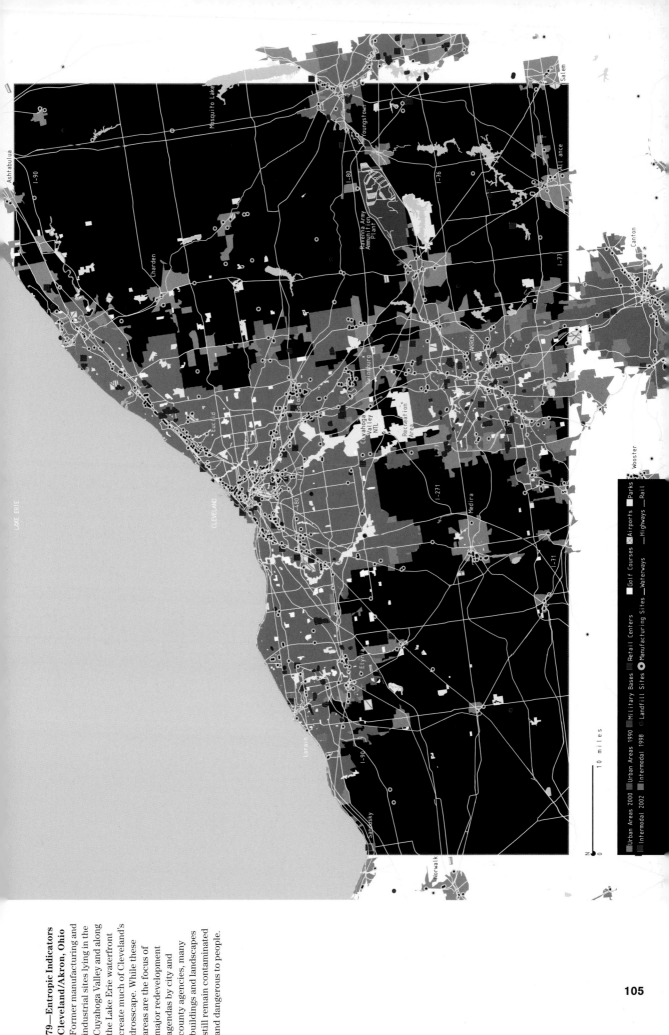

**79—Entropic Indicators
Cleveland/Akron, Ohio**
Former manufacturing and
industrial sites lying in the
Cuyahoga Valley and along
the Lake Erie waterfront
create much of Cleveland's
drosscape. While these
areas are the focus of
major redevelopment
agendas by city and
county agencies, many
buildings and landscapes
still remain contaminated
and dangerous to people.

Urban Areas 2000 Urban Areas 1990 Military Bases Retail Centers Golf Courses Airports Parks
Intermodal 2002 Intermodal 1998 Landfill Sites Manufacturing Sites Waterways Highways Rail

10 miles

N
0

LAKE ERIE

Ashtabula

I-90

Charden

Mosquito Lake

Youngstown

I-80

I-76

Alliance

Ravenna Army
Ammunition
Plant

I-77

Canton

Euclid

Solon

Winsburg

Cuyahoga
Valley
NTL

Recreation
Area

AKRON

Wooster

CLEVELAND

I-480

I-271

Medira

I-71

Elyria

I-90

Lorain

Sandusky

Norwalk

Salem

105

**80—Housing around
Kent State University
Airport, Summit County,
Akron, Ohio**

Agricultural land
surrounded this Akron
airport when it was built
in 1917. Today the airport
is abutted by big box retail
and residential housing
developments.

**81—Dispersal Graph
Cleveland/Akron, Ohio**
Unlike many other
urbanized areas adjacent
to water, the Cleveland
region exhibits linear
growth (rather than
concentric) away from
its center, most notably
(quad 4, transect 4)
towards Akron.

107

**82—Solon Industrial
Park, Cuyahoga
County, Ohio**
Industrial agglomerations
are the manifestation
of a post-Fordist
economy and decreasing
transportation costs.
Cuyahoga County's
historic association with
rubber manufacturing
enterprises has changed
to make room for high
technology and plastics
and polymer industries.

83—Spindle Chart
Cleveland/Akron, Ohio

From 1977 to 2001
Cuyahoga County
(Cleveland's central
county) was the only area
in the region with a net
loss of manufacturing
establishments. Gains
in manufacturing
establishments have
occurred in every other
county up to seventy miles
from the city center.

Change In Manufacturing Establishments + Distance From Center

Manufacturing Establishments Change, 1977–1992
Manufacturing Establishments Growth, 1992–2001
Manufacturing Establishments Decline, 1992–2001

COUNTY RANKING:
1977–2001

	% Change in Manufacturing Est.	Distance from Center (mi.)
TUSCAWARAS	22%	72.3
CARROLL	3%	68.5
COLUMBIANA	2%	68.0
HOLMES	153%	64.4
MAHONING	17%	57.4
ASHTABULA	10%	50.8
STARK	9%	49.6
WAYNE	49%	46.9
PORTAGE	55%	33.1
LAKE	56%	28.2
MEDINA	57%	27.4
LORAIN	22%	27.4
GEAUGA	48%	26.1
SUMMIT	22%	25.0
CUYAHOGA	-30%	0

N

500

272

100

-100

-500

1108

40 miles

75 miles

LAKE 43
22
20
229 51 4
CUYAHOGA 655
0
SUMMIT 230
4 31 22
60 85 63
1 29 24
7 18
-64 70 80 84 -32 58 50 -25 -6

CUYAHOGA
LAKE
GEAUGA
ASHTABULA
PORTAGE
SUMMIT
MAHONING
COLUMBIANA
STARK
CARROLL
TUSCAWARAS
MEDINA
WAYNE
HOLMES
ASHLAND
LORAIN
ERIE
HURON

Old Central Sites
(Cuyahoga County)

New Peripheral Sites
(Portage/Summit County)

Dallas/
Fort Worth

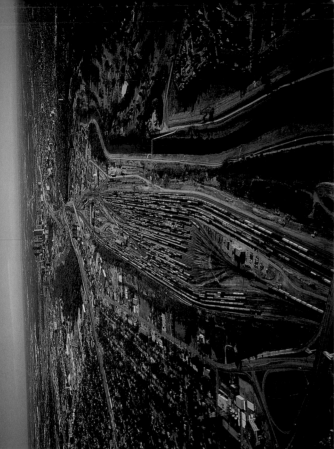

84—South Side, Dallas, Texas (left) Over $1 billion is invested in the phased redevelopment of the Trinity River Corridor (far left). Trinity is the industrial manufacturing area of Dallas. The former Sears Roebuck and Company Merchandising Center, now a brownfield site, is in the foreground (center).

85—Centennial Yard, Union Pacific, Fort Worth, Texas (right) Companies such as RadioShack Corp. and Pier 1 Imports are locating headquarters along the Trinity River Corridor in Fort Worth. Their manufacturing operations, however, are moving to China. Union Pacific's transfer station (foreground) moves goods from the West Coast to East Coast markets.

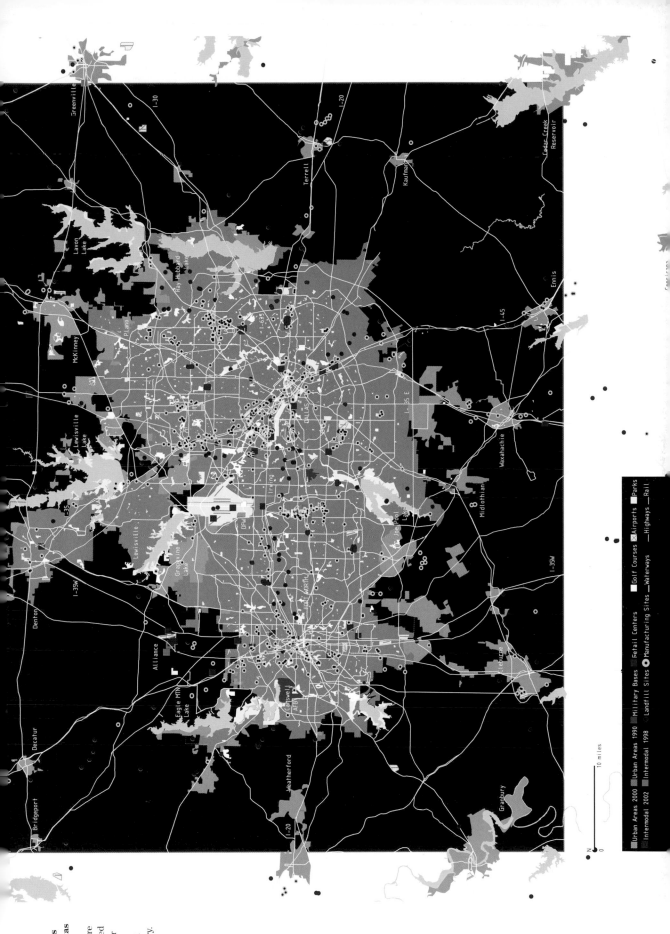

**86—Entropic Indicators
Dallas/Fort Worth, Texas**
This region exhibits a
classic drosscape signature
with the majority of wasted
deindustrialized land near
the city center and the
wasteful low density land
around the city's periphery.

Urban Areas 2000 Urban Areas 1990 Military Bases Retail Centers Golf Courses Airports Parks
Intermodal 2002 Intermodal 1998 Landfill Sites Manufacturing Sites Waterways Highways Rail

10 miles

N

111

87—Plano, Texas
Plano almost doubled its population from 1990 to 2003, surging from 128,713 to 237,950 residents. Quality high technology jobs and various company headquarters located in the North Dallas region are major reasons for this growth.

88—Dispersal Graph
Dallas / Fort Worth, Texas
Population density declines
sharply within a ten-mile
radius from the city center
in all four quads measured.
Growth outward from
the city center is mostly
continuous with few zones
of very low density (black)
between urbanized areas.

Central Cities
Urbanized Areas, 1990
Urbanized Areas, 2000
Approx. Urbanized Extent, 1950

persons/sq. mi.

32,708

20,000

10,000

0_DALLAS

10

20

40

50

60

70   miles

1950 Approx. Urbanized Extent

FORT WORTH

DALLAS

Abilene

Wichita Falls

Denton

Denison

Richardson/Pla...

Tyler

Longview

Bryan

Temple

Waco

Killeen

OKLAHOMA
ARKANSAS

N

Quad 1

Quad 4

Quad 3

Quad 2

transect 1

transect 2

transect 3

transect 4

0

70 miles

40 miles

89—Perot Systems World Headquarters along President George Bush Turnpike, Plano/Richardson, Collin County, Texas

Perot Systems, Texas Instruments (TI), and many other telecommunications and electronics industries are located in the North Dallas region. In 1958, TI developed the integrated circuit here. TI is building a 1-million-square-foot silicon wafer fabrication facility, its third in the last decade.

Change in Manufacturing Establishments + Distance from Center

Manufacturing Establishments Change, 1977-1992
Manufacturing Establishments Growth, 1992-2001
Manufacturing Establishments Decline, 1992-2001

90—Spindle Chart
Dallas/Fort Worth, Texas
Except for minor losses in two counties, including central Dallas County, this region has experienced large gains in manufacturing establishments. Hood County, sixty-five miles from the city center, grew 191 percent.

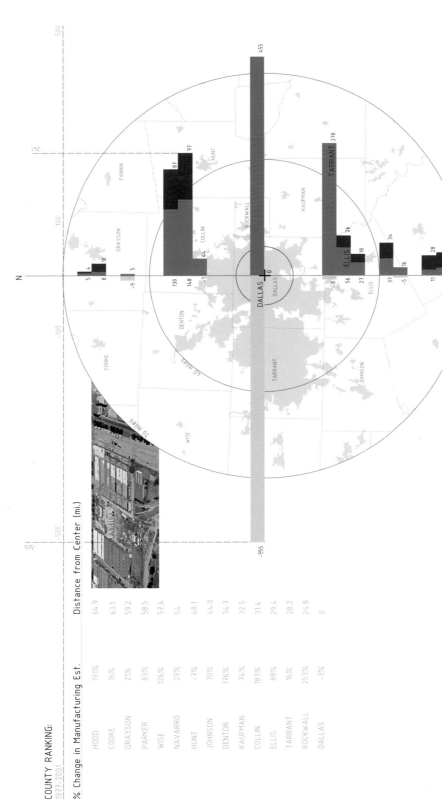

COUNTY RANKING:
1977-2001

	% Change in Manufacturing Est.	Distance from Center (mi.)
HOOD	191%	64.9
COOKE	16%	63.1
GRAYSON	21%	59.2
PARKER	83%	58.5
WISE	126%	57.4
NAVARRO	29%	54
HUNT	-7%	48.1
JOHNSON	70%	44.0
DENTON	176%	34.7
KAUFMAN	74%	32.5
COLLIN	187%	31.4
ELLIS	88%	29.4
TARRANT	16%	28.2
ROCKWALL	253%	24.8
DALLAS	-3%	0

New Peripheral Sites
(near Collin County)

Old Central Sites
(Dallas County)

Denver/
Front Range

**91—South Platte
River Corridor,
Denver, Colorado**

Approximately 65 percent
of Colorado's population
lives along a thirty-mile
wide territory running
along the South Platte
River. Throughout
the twentieth century,
heavy industrial and
landfilling activities
concentrated within this
area. New education and
entertainment complexes
such as the Invesco Field
at Mile High (stadium),
Pepsi Center, Coors
Field, and University
of Colorado at Denver
are transforming
the landscape.

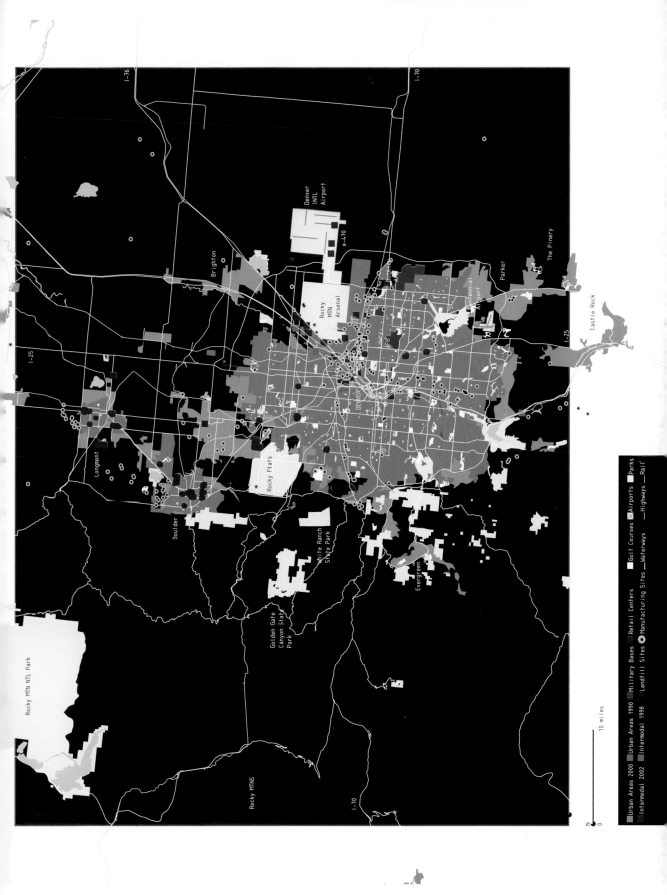

**92—Entropic Indicators
Denver/Front Range,
Colorado**

This region exhibits a
classic drosscape signature
with the majority of wasted
deindustrialized land
near the city center and
the wasteful low-density
land around the city's
periphery. The appearance
of abundant park space
is deceiving due to Rocky
Flats and Rocky Mountain
Arsenal, which were both
recently converted from
toxic industrial sites to
"wildlife areas."

Rocky MTN NTL Park

I-76

I-70

Denver
INTL
Airport

e-470

Brighton

Rocky
MTN
Arsenal

Burlington

Centennial
Airport

Parker

The Pinery

Castle Rock

I-25

DENVER

AFB

I-25

Longmont

Boulder

Rocky Flats

White Ranch
State Park

Evergreen

Golden Gate
Canyon State
Park

Rocky MTNS

I-70

10 miles

N

Urban Areas 2000 · Urban Areas 1990 · Military Bases · Retail Centers · Golf Courses · ✕ Airports · ▪ Parks
▪ Intermodal 2002 · Intermodal 1998 · Landfill Sites · ⊙ Manufacturing Sites · Waterways · Highways · Rail'

117

93—Boulder County, Colorado
Population density is nearly 360 persons per square mile in Boulder County. In Denver County, density is ten times that number, or just under 3,600 persons per square mile.

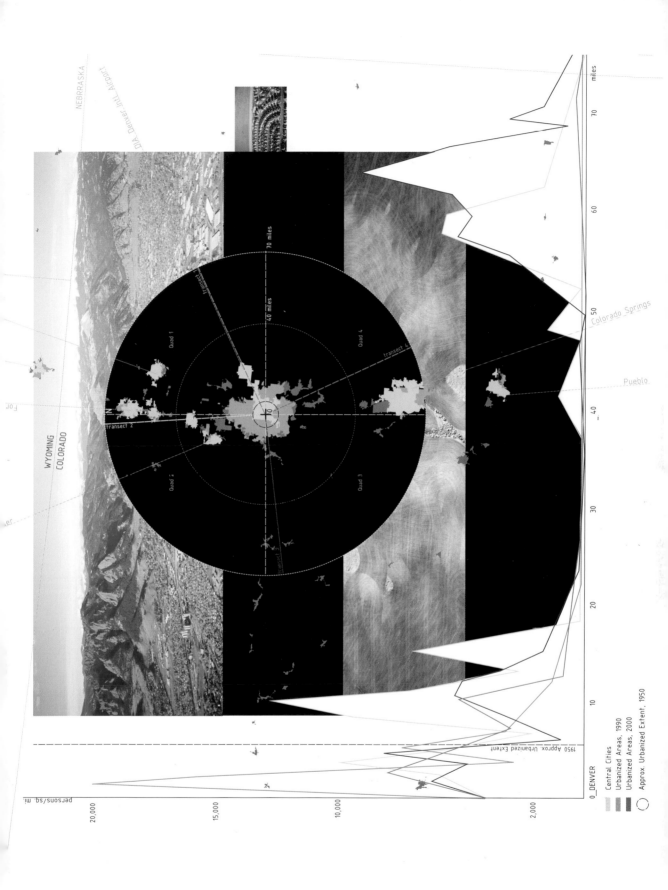

**94—Dispersal Graph
Denver / Front Range,
Colorado**

The Denver Front Range
region is characterized
by alternating peaks of
moderate density and
valleys of very low density
roughly every thirty miles
along Interstate 25.

Central Cities
Urbanized Areas, 1990
Urbanized Areas, 2000
Approx. Urbanized Extent, 1950

persons/sq. mi.
20,000
15,000
10,000
2,000

0_DENVER

miles

WYOMING
COLORADO
NEBRASKA

DIA_Denver Intl Airport

Colorado_Springs
Pueblo

1950 Approx. Urbanized Extent

95—Rocky Mountain Steel Mills, Pueblo County, Colorado
This steel mill is one of the last two remaining U.S. producers of railroad products. Recent growth in international trade catalyzed new rail construction (and repair) in the Western U.S. The City of Pueblo is in the background.

96—Spindle Chart
Denver/Front Range, Colorado

Since 1977, central Denver County lost 22 percent of its manufacturing establishments. Douglas County and Park County (twenty-five miles south and sixty-two miles southeast of central Denver, respectively) both had manufacturing gains over 400 percent.

Manufacturing Establishments Change, 1977–1992
Manufacturing Establishments Growth, 1992–2001
Manufacturing Establishments Decline, 1992–2001

COUNTY RANKING:
1977–2001

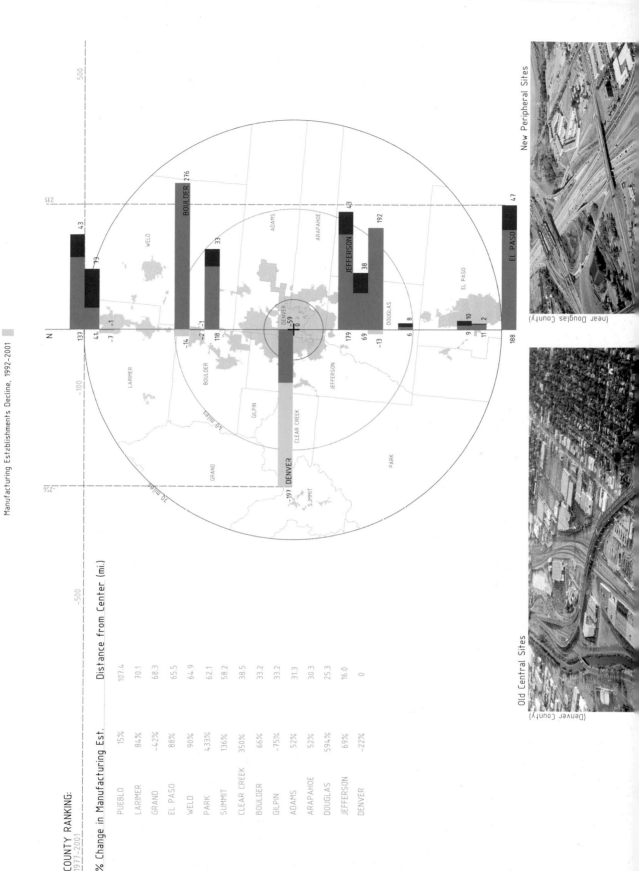

% Change in Manufacturing Est.	Distance from Center (mi.)
PUEBLO 15%	107.4
LARIMER 84%	70.1
GRAND -4.2%	68.3
EL PASO 88%	65.5
WELD 90%	64.9
PARK 433%	62.1
SUMMIT 136%	58.2
CLEAR CREEK 350%	38.5
BOULDER 66%	33.2
GILPIN -75%	33.2
ADAMS 52%	31.3
ARAPAHOE 52%	30.3
DOUGLAS 594%	25.3
JEFFERSON 69%	16.0
DENVER -22%	0

Old Central Sites
(Denver County)

New Peripheral Sites
(near Douglas County)

Houston

97—Englewood Yards, downtown Houston, Harris County, Texas
Union Pacific's Houston complex employs 2,250 people with an annual payroll of $132 million (2002). Major commodities transported here include petroleum products, chemicals, export grain, gravel and aggregates, automobiles and automobile parts, paper, glass, coal, and general merchandise. Rolling through this complex daily, 165 trains serve southern Texas, the neighboring Ship Channel, and the Port of Houston.

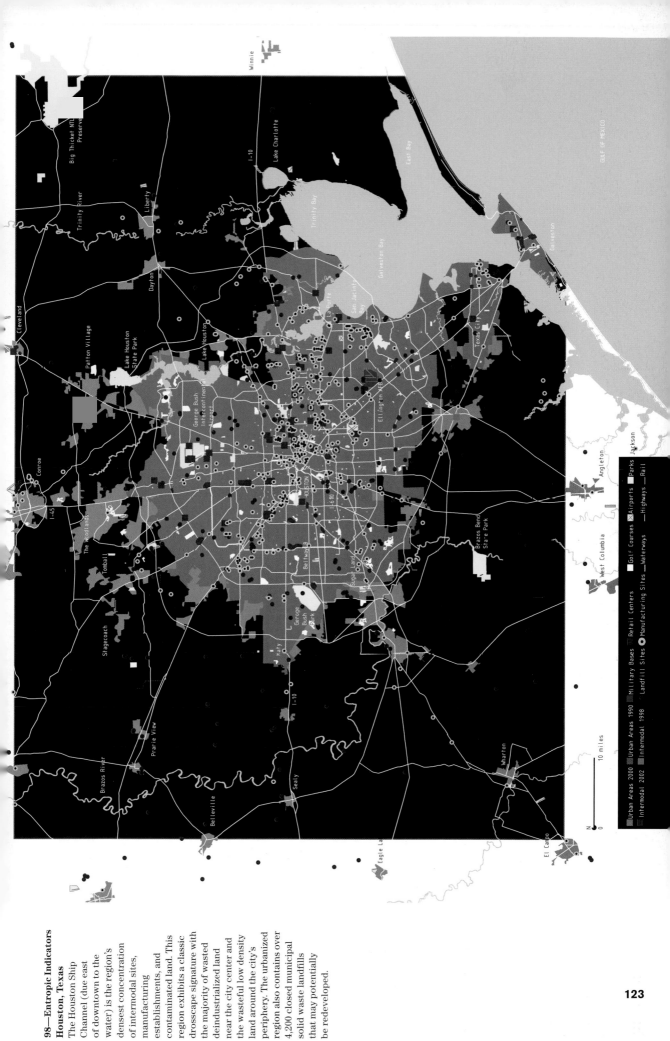

**98—Entropic Indicators
Houston, Texas**

The Houston Ship
Channel (due east
of downtown to the
water) is the region's
densest concentration
of intermodal sites,
manufacturing
establishments, and
contaminated land. This
region exhibits a classic
drosscape signature with
the majority of wasted
deindustrialized land
near the city center and
the wasteful low density
land around the city's
periphery. The urbanized
region also contains over
4,200 closed municipal
solid waste landfills
that may potentially
be redeveloped.

Urban Areas 2000   Urban Areas 1990   Military Bases   Retail Centers   Golf Courses   Airports   Parks   Jackson
Intermodal 2002   Intermodal 1998   Landfill Sites   Manufacturing Sites   Highways   Rail
                                                                           Waterways

N
0   10 miles

99—Missouri City, Fort Bend County, looking toward Houston, Texas

Population in Fort Bend County from 1990 through 2000 increased 57 percent. Missouri City grew at a 46 percent rate while nearby Sugar Land swelled by 128 percent, making it the second fastest growing city in Texas. The Texas Medical Center's skyline is recognizable just right of downtown. The Medical Center employs over 65,400 people (many of whom live in Fort Bend County) and contains 44,188 parking spaces.

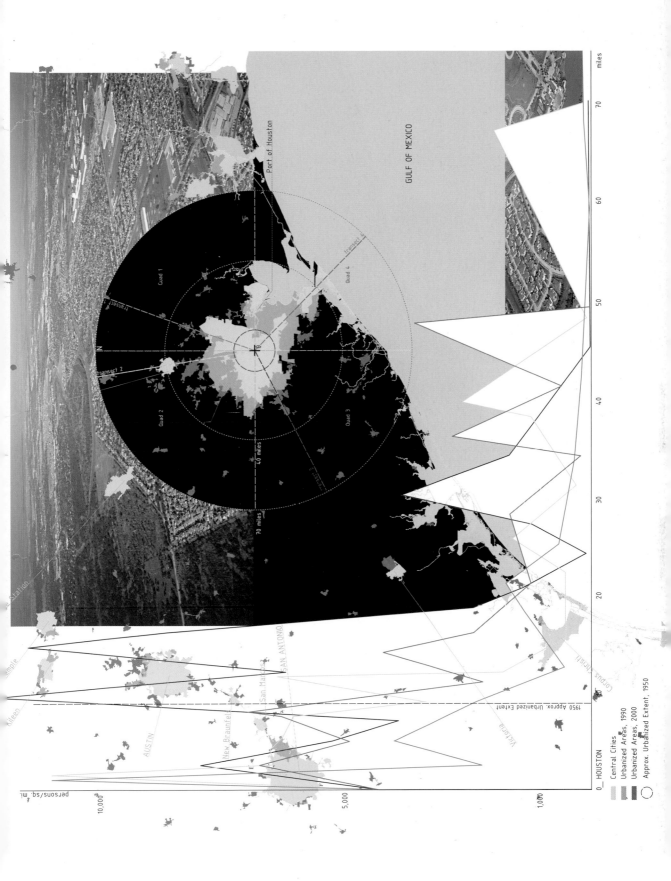

**100—Dispersal Graph
Houston, Texas**
Population density is
relatively high in all four
quads measured, up to a
twenty-mile radius from
the city center.

Central Cities
Urbanized Areas, 1990
Urbanized Areas, 2000
Approx. Urbanized Extent, 1950

persons/sq. mi.
10,000
5,000
1,000

0_ HOUSTON

miles
70
60
50
40
30
20
10

GULF OF MEXICO

Port of Houston

Quad 1
Quad 2
Quad 3
Quad 4

40 miles
70 miles

Transect 2
Transect 1

AUSTIN
SAN ANTONIO
New Braunfels
San Marcos
Victoria
Temple
Killeen
Station
Corpus Christi

1950 Approx. Urbanized Extent

101—Intersection of I-290 at Beltway 8, Harris County, Cypress/Fairbanks, Texas
Houston's northwest quadrant holds 72 percent of current warehouse construction. The northwest's industrial market has over 58 million square feet, with an occupancy rate of over 92 percent.

Manufacturing Establishments Change, 1977–1992
Manufacturing Establishments Growth, 1992–2001
Manufacturing Establishments Decline, 1992–2001

102—Spindle Chart
Houston, Texas

Houston's central Harris County is one of the few major city centers in the U.S. that have maintained an increase in manufacturing establishments since 1977. Other counties with impressive gains are Fort Bend, Montgomery, and Waller Counties, all located beyond thirty miles from central Houston.

COUNTY RANKING:
1977–2001

	% Change in Manufacturing Est.	Distance from Center (mi.)
COLORADO	58%	72.8
WASHINGTON	70%	70.8
JEFFERSON	-6%	69.8
HARDIN	-7%	67.8
AUSTIN	44%	56.0
SAN JACINTO	-18%	53.9
CHAMBERS	100%	45.3
WALLER	250%	43.4
BRAZORIA	50%	42.3
LIBERTY	-22%	39.9
MONTGOMERY	264.3%	38.9
FORT BEND	309%	32.6
GALVESTON	32%	31.3
HARRIS	14.%	0

New Peripheral Sites
(Northwest Harris County)

Old Central Sites
(East Harris County)

Los Angeles

**103—Downtown
intermodal transfer
facility, Los Angeles,
California**
Urban traffic congestion
has forced railroad and
trucking transportation
companies to restructure
their routing procedures
and networks. Goods
that previously passed
through central urban
areas by train or truck
now bypass the city.
This creates tremendous
gains in efficiency.

**104—Entropic Indicators
Los Angeles, California**
Only 20 to 30 percent
of all space designated
for industrial use in
Los Angeles County is
actually used for industrial
purposes. The remaining
bulk of industrial buildings
and land has either
been adaptively reused
or is abandoned.

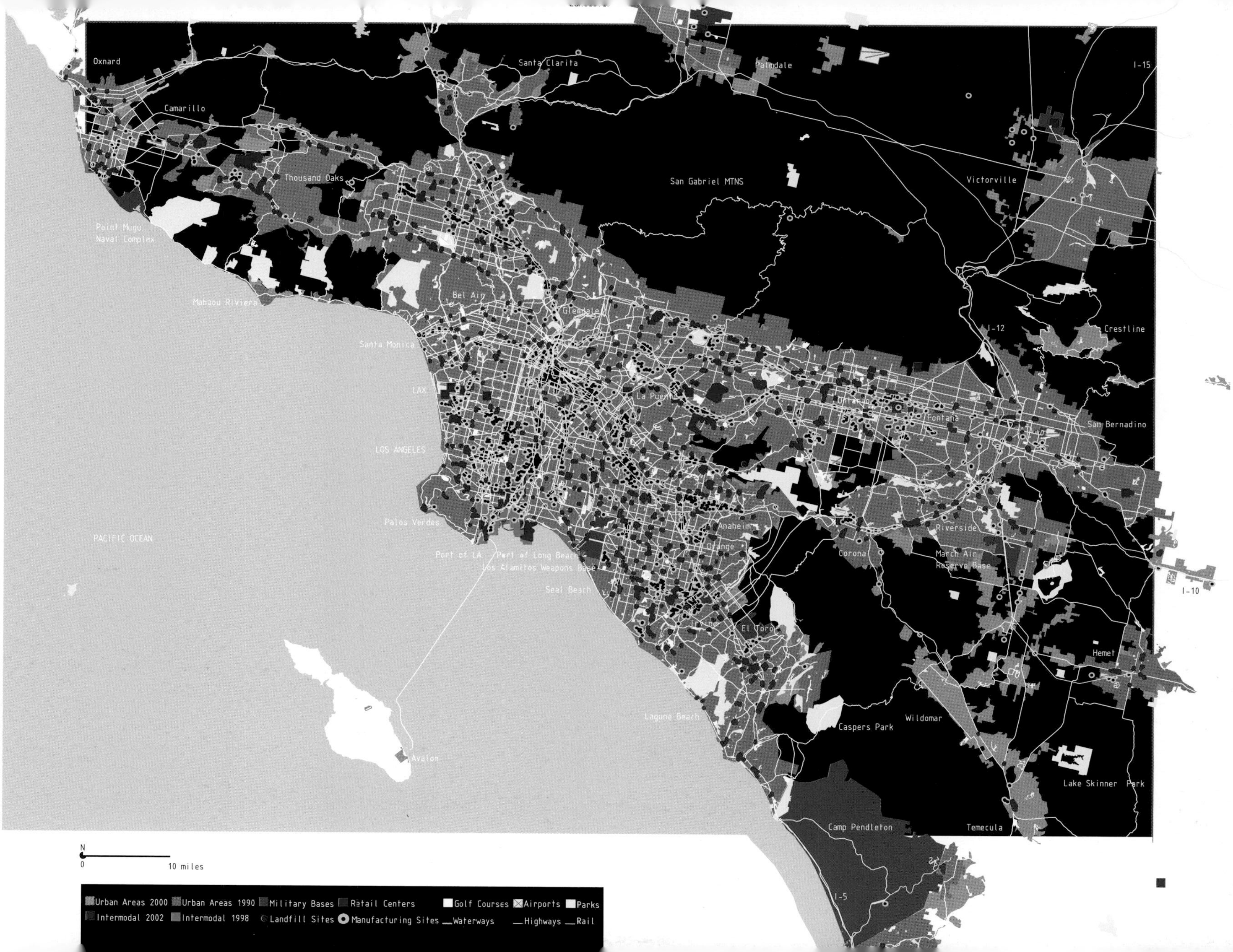

Urban Areas 2000 · Urban Areas 1990 · Military Bases · Retail Centers · Golf Courses · Parks

Intermodal 2002 · Intermodal 1998 · Landfill Sites · Manufacturing Sites · Highways · Rail

Waterways

N

0   10 miles

105—Rancho Cucamonga, San Bernardino County, California

Rancho Cucamonga is located about forty-five miles west of Los Angeles and seventy-five miles north of Long Beach. The San Gabriel Mountains and the San Bernardino National Forest lie to its north. From 1991 to 2000 employment grew by 76.8 percent and retail jobs grew by 45.4 percent. Manufacturing, distribution, and transportation sectors account for 36.5 percent of the city's job growth.

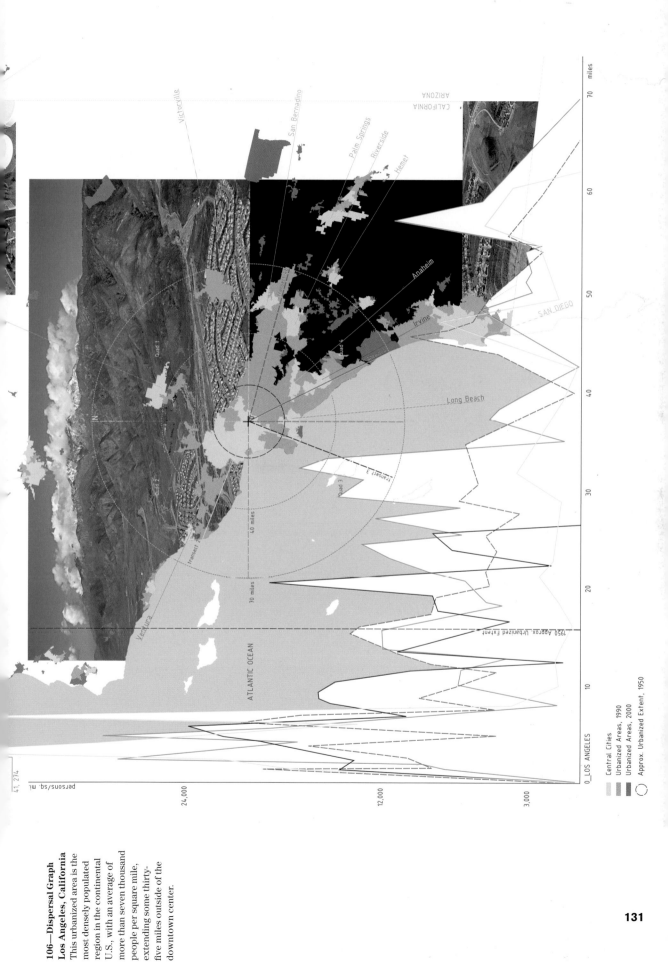

106—Dispersal Graph
Los Angeles, California
This urbanized area is the most densely populated region in the continental U.S., with an average of more than seven thousand people per square mile, extending some thirty-five miles outside of the downtown center.

41, 274

persons/sq. mi.

24,000

12,000

3,000

Central Cities
Urbanized Areas, 1990
Urbanized Areas, 2000
Approx. Urbanized Extent, 1950

0_LOS ANGELES

10   20   30   40   50   60   70   miles

1950 Approx. Urbanized Extent

Victorville

San Bernardino

Palm Springs

Riverside

Hemet

CALIFORNIA
ARIZONA

Anaheim

Irvine

SAN DIEGO

Long Beach

ATLANTIC OCEAN

Ventura

N

40 miles

70 miles

Quad 1

Quad 2

Quad 3

Quad 4

Transect 1

Transect 3

107—South of Ontario International Airport, San Bernardino County, California

The Inland Empire is located in southwestern San Bernardino County. The U.S. Department of Commerce estimates this region has a $51 billion economy, which is large enough to classify it as the thirty-second largest state.¹ This includes cargo operations, warehousing and manufacturing facilities, and the densest concentration of steel manufacturing in California. Every major trucking firm in Southern California brings its cargo to this area for sorting into full containers before it is shipped cross-country or internationally.

Change In Manufacturing Establishments + Distance From Center

108—Spindle Chart
Los Angeles, California

Central Los Angeles
County has lost 17 percent
of its manufacturing
establishments since 1977.
During the same period
Ventura County and
Riverside County (50 miles
and 138 miles from the
center, respectively) have
each increased more than
100 percent.

Manufacturing Establishments Change, 1977–1992
Manufacturing Establishments Growth, 1992–2001
Manufacturing Establishments Decline, 1992–2001

N

COUNTY RANKING:
1977–2001

% Change in Manufacturing Est.		Distance from Center (mi.)
RIVERSIDE	124%	137.9
SAN BERNADINO	117%	137.4
SAN DIEGO	74%	117.8
KERN	15%	90.8
VENTURA	101%	50.9
ORANGE	22%	39.8
LOS ANGELES	-17%	0

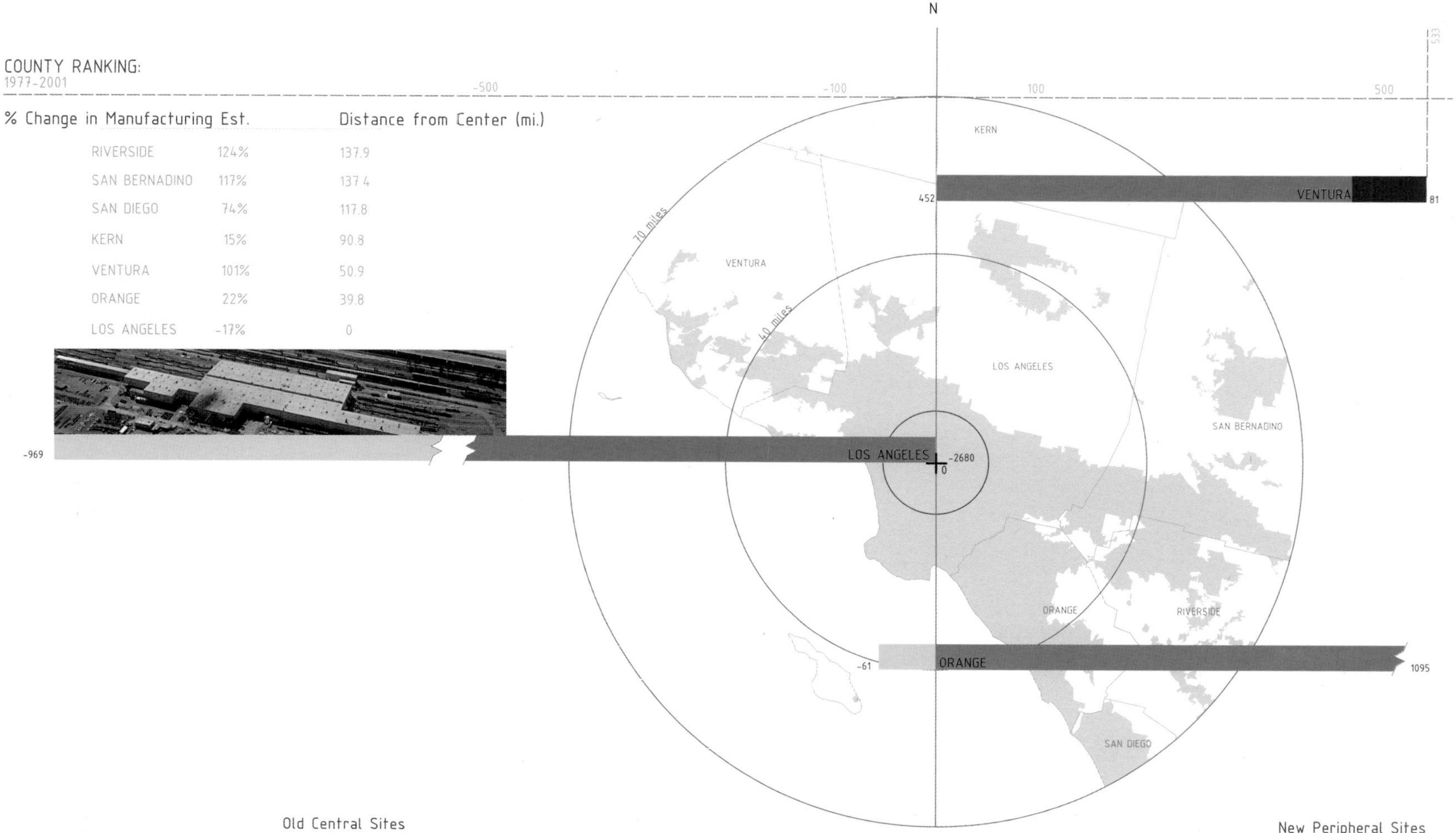

500

100

-100

-500

VENTURA — 81

452

-2680

0

LOS ANGELES

ORANGE

-61

1095

-969

SAN BERNADINO

RIVERSIDE

SAN DIEGO

KERN

LOS ANGELES

VENTURA

50 miles

70 miles

Old Central Sites

(Los Angeles County)

New Peripheral Sites

(San Bernadino County)

133

Phoenix

109—Van Buren Street, West Phoenix, Maricopa County, Arizona
Infrastructural land development is rarely linear and is often associated with global-scale socio-economic dynamics. For example, the Union Pacific Railroad line in this image, a branch line from Los Angeles, connects to Phoenix's Sky Harbor International Airport and its cargo facilities (in the background). Whether the line remains or transforms into a main trunk line is determined by profitability, local politics, and global logistics.

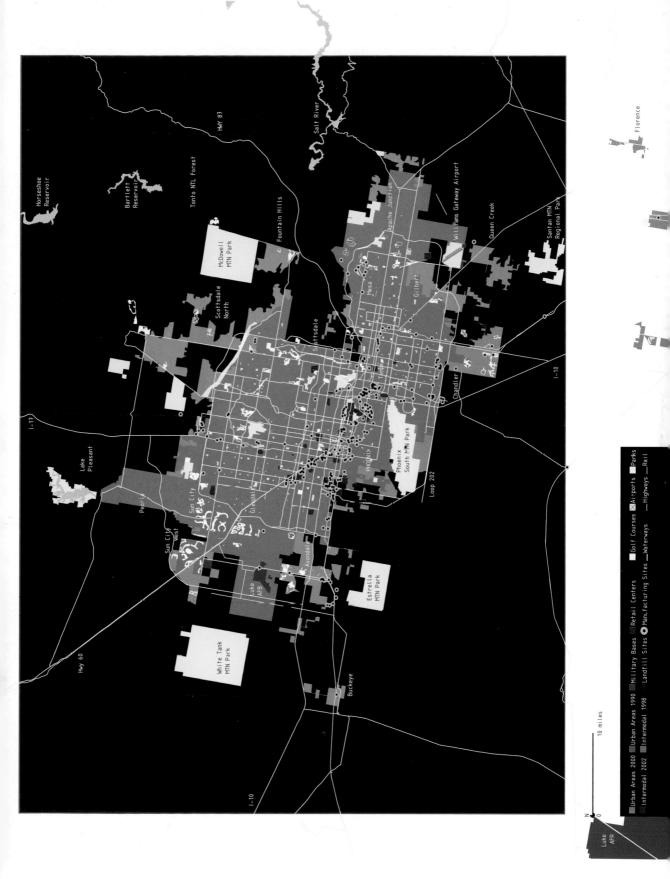

110—Entropic Indicators
Phoenix, Arizona
Industrial and
manufacturing sites are
concentrated east of
downtown and along the
Interstate 60 corridor.
With relatively few old
industrial sites, the
majority of drosscape
in this region is created
by wasteful land-use
practices in outlying areas.

Urban Areas 2000   Urban Areas 1990   Military Bases   Retail Centers   Golf Courses   Airports   Parks
Intermodal 2002   Intermodal 1998   Landfill Sites   Manufacturing Sites   Waterways   Highways   Rail

10 miles

111—Housing adjacent to South Mountain Park, Phoenix, Maricopa County, Arizona.
Cities in the Greater Phoenix area attempt to keep pace with population growth by annexing land on the periphery. This region has grown from 17 square miles in 1950 to 473 square miles in 2000. So-called "snowbirds," or residents who only live here in the winter months, occupy large amounts of land in the form of detached residential units. At least 250,000 people from the midwestern and northeastern states winter in the Greater Phoenix area annually.

**112—Dispersal Graph
Phoenix, Arizona**

Quad 3 (southwest) has the least amount of newly urbanized land due to an impeding mountain range and indian reservation.

Central Cities
Urbanized Areas, 1990
Urbanized Areas, 2000
Approx. Urbanized Extent, 1950

113—Chandler high-tech cluster, Maricopa County, Arizona
In the Greater Phoenix area, 631 high-tech firms employ more than 49,000 people.

138

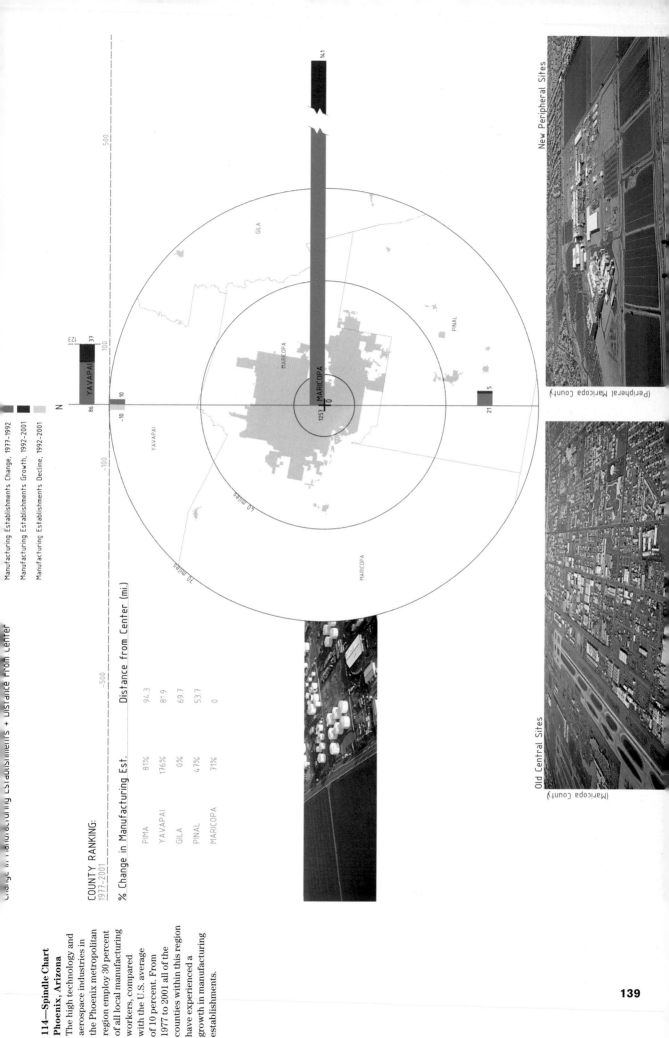

114—Spindle Chart
Phoenix, Arizona

The high technology and aerospace industries in the Phoenix metropolitan region employ 30 percent of all local manufacturing workers, compared with the U.S. average of 10 percent. From 1977 to 2001 all of the counties within this region have experienced a growth in manufacturing establishments.

Change in Manufacturing Establishments + Distance From Center

■ Manufacturing Establishments Change, 1977–1992
■ Manufacturing Establishments Growth, 1992–2001
▨ Manufacturing Establishments Decline, 1992–2001

N

COUNTY RANKING:
1977–2001

% Change in Manufacturing Est.	Distance from Center (mi.)
PIMA	81%	94.3
YAVAPAI	176%	81.9
GILA	0%	69.7
PINAL	4.7%	53.7
MARICOPA	71%	0

Distance from Center (mi.)

-500   -100   -10   10   100   500

141
123   37
86
10
-10
21   5
1257   0
MARICOPA

GILA
PINAL
MARICOPA
YAVAPAI

40 miles
10 miles

Old Central Sites
(Maricopa County)

New Peripheral Sites
(Peripheral Maricopa County)

Chapter Four
Waste Landscapes

Waste Landscapes of Dwelling (LODs)
The wealthy can afford to be wasteful...
–Susan Strasser, *Waste and Want: A Social History of Trash*

Waste landscapes of dwelling (LODs) refer to voids of
land integrally designed into housing developments,
especially into walled or gated enclaves. These voids
often have singular programmatic intentions (golf course,
buffer zone, preservation area, trail system, etc.). Mostly
occupants who have invested in a given residential
community use them. There are two types of LOD voids:
those outside and inside the enclave. "Outside" voids
encircle the enclave as buffers and separators from
adjacent development or other possible "nuisance"
land uses that may adversely affect the quality of life,
or "values," held by the dwellers of the enclave. Other
voids such as thickly planted areas or topography
unsuitable for building are planned as protection
systems. Some voids are designed pragmatically, for
example, to allow for public utility easements that cross
through enclave territory. "Inside" voids are typically
spread throughout the development. They serve the
social (privacy and entertainment), circulation, and
recreation needs of its inhabitants.
      Outside and inside voids manifest themselves at
varying scales. An outside void may appear between
two developments within close proximity of one another
to enable a sharing of void space, or a controlled
separation, between subdivision areas (see figures 115,
116). Moreover, the outside void may be configured as
a vast space whereby isolation and distance are the
planned intentions of a subdivision. Inside voids work in a
similar manner but at smaller scales, such as lot location,
orientation, and parcel size. A lot's location (corner lots,
cul-de-sac lots, and lots with views being more valuable)
and it's proximity to amenities characterize the design,
orchestrated marketing, and valuing of an enclave's inside
void (see figures 117, 118, 119, 120).
      The best illustration of an LOD is the golf course.
From 1970 to 2003 the number of golf courses in the U.S.
increased from 7,516 to 15,899.[1] At the end of 2002 there
were 1203 eighteen-hole equivalents in the construction
pipeline, including 408 under construction, 376 in planning,
and 419 proposed.[2] About 46 percent of the golf holes
currently under construction will be part of a residential
community.[3] All of this construction might lead one to
assume that more golf rounds are played than ever before.
This is not the case. Since 2000, when golf playing peaked
at 518 million rounds, golf course construction and
golf rounds played in the U.S. have steadily decreased.[4]
In 2002 a record number of fifty golf courses declared
bankruptcy, foreclosed, or were sold or converted to other

[1] Statistical Abstract of the United States 2003, Section 26: Arts,
Entertainment, and Recreation, No. 1230–1264. U.S. Census Bureau.
[2] Ibid.
[3] Ibid.
[4] Ibid.

uses. More than four hundred courses (about 20 percent of the courses built per year during the early 2000s) are for sale, at prices greatly reduced from the actual construction costs.[5] These trends suggest that golf courses are producing waste landscape both through a decrease in use density and through fiscal failure.

Residential "golf spaces" are a well-known marketing tool of home developers, who use them to demand higher prices, in the form of lot premiums, for the lots they sell (see figures 121, 122).[6] Less well known is the fate of golf courses developed in conjunction with residential communities. Many golf courses planned within residential communities initially operate at a loss. The lot premiums charged at the time of purchase help offset these losses (as do tax write-offs). So once the golf course community is built-out and sold, golf course ownership or management shifts to the residents or private companies.[7] Over time, maintenance and tax costs become a burden on these entities. As a result, many golf courses experience financial difficulties, then fall into disrepair or get converted to other uses.

115

116

117

118

119

120

121

122

[5] Ibid. Also see "Two Moore County Golf Courses In 'Rough' File For Bankruptcy," *Raleigh-Durham, Fayetteville, North Carolina's WRAL-TV5*, http://www.wral.com/news/3426927/detail.html (accessed June 16, 2004). In Tokyo, Japan, the number of golfers is down 20 percent since 1990, and nearly 1,700 courses have been forced into bankruptcy, including twenty-three in the first half of this year.

[6] R.E. Somol, "Join The Club," *Wired*, (June 2003): 163.

[7] Jonathan R. Laing, "Golf's Prospects Dim Despite Bright Hopes," *Wall Street Journal Guide to Property, Real Estate Journal*, August 15, 2003, http://www.realestatejournal.com/propertyreport/newsandtrends/20030815-laing.html (accessed August 25, 2004).

115—Housing along the south side of Phoenix South Mountain Park, Chandler / Phoenix, Arizona
Outside voids may appear between nearby developments, thus enabling a sharing of void-space,
or controlled separation, between subdivision areas.

116—Housing at The Colony / Frisco, Texas, north of Plano
Outside voids encircle the enclave as buffers and separators from adjacent development and other
possible "nuisance" land uses that may adversely affect the quality of life or "values" held by dwellers
of the enclave. Outside voids may be temporary as new development infills the voids over time.

117—Housing at Scottsdale, Arizona   **14**
Inside voids work at smaller scales (than outside voids), such as lot location, orientation, and parcel size.
They serve the social (privacy and entertainment) needs of the inhabitants.

118—Fly-in housing near Joliet, Illinois
Residents use airplane taxiways in their backyards to access the grass runway at the top of the image.
Planes are stored in hangars next to each home. Inside voids serve the circulation and recreation needs
of the inhabitants.

119—Trailer housing at Interstate Highways 10/60, Sun City West / Glendale, Arizona
With transportable housing such as mobile homes and trailers, the inside voids are trailer parking
spaces, and the outside voids are the places to be explored on wheels.

120—Canal housing near Irvine, California
The inside void is water for the recreation needs of the inhabitants.

153

121—Golf course housing along Pacific Coast Highway, near Newport Coast / Laguna Beach, California
The outside void is created with a golf course. Lots with direct access and views to the ocean and golf
course are part of the orchestrated marketing and valuing of an enclave's inside and outside voids.

122—Golf course housing in Scottsdale, Arizona
The private golf course is an exclusive inside void.

Waste Landscapes of Transition (LOTs)

All waste is traded.
–Richard Porter, *The Economics of Waste*

Waste landscapes of transition (LOTs) reveal the transitory nature of capital investment and real-estate speculation. Some LOTs are intentionally designed and built as transitional land uses, such as staging areas, storage yards, parking surfaces, transfer stations, etc. Others act as a holding ground until real-estate values increase (see figures 123, 124, 125).

The mechanism most responsible for the production of these LOTs is real estate investment trusts (REITs). An REIT is a company that finances, owns, and sometimes operates real estate. It pays at least 90 percent of its taxable income to shareholders annually in the form of dividends.[8] In 1960 the U.S. Congress created REITs to provide citizens with the ability to invest in large-scale commercial-property development. Today there are about 180 REITs publicly traded on major stock exchanges. They have assets of more than $375 billion. REITs invest in a variety of property types: shopping centers, apartments, warehouses, office buildings, and hotels, to name a few. Most specialize in one property type, like the shopping mall (see figure 126), car dealership, gas station, or factory outlet center.[9] They profit by selling or renting building space or by improving property, which usually increases the land's value.

Self-storage facilities are one of the newer types of REIT investments (see figure 127). Since the early 1990s, self-storage REITs have assisted in the creation of thousands of easily identifiable facilities that are located along America's roadways. On average, self-storage facilities make net profits of about 60 to 70 percent occupancy (largely due to low building and operating costs).[10] This is incentive for using REIT investor capital to build an excess of self-storage facilities. Through this process the REIT may profit from the increased land values, even though the actual property is not fully utilized. It is easy for one to imagine that any self-storage facility is merely a "holder" for future (i.e., more profitable) forms of development, like office space or housing. This is particularly true in new-growth regions, where there is an abundant supply of land. The nation's two largest self-storage REITs are Public Storage and Shurgard. Combined, these companies own more than two thousand facilities in forty states and eighty U.S. cities. They offer more than 110 million square feet of rentable space; their market capitalization (the total value of all the shares of stock) is nearly $7 billion.[11]

[8] New York Stock Exchange.
[9] The National Association of Real Estate Investment Trusts (REITs).
[10] Self Storage Association.
[11] Marc A. Boorstein, "The Self-Storage REITs: A Survey of Three Major Players," *Inside Self-Storage Magazine*, February 2004. Also see Shurgard Storage, Inc. official web site, http://www.shurgard.com; Public Storage, Inc. official web site, http://www.publicstorage.com; and Pubilc Storage, Inc. official business parks web site, http://www.psbusinessparks.com.

123

124

125

126

127

123—Inman Yard, Norfolk Southern Railroad, Atlanta, Georgia

Inman consists of five yards that classify, forward, and receive local destination and intermodal shipments. Within twenty-four hours it handles 108 trains with 8,640 cars. Hundreds of older intermodal hubs in the U.S. are being transformed into new land uses as the result of changes in distribution and manufacturing networks.

124—Texas Stadium, Irving, Texas
Home of the NFL's Dallas Cowboys, city officials are looking to redevelop this site when the Cowboys
leave in 2009 for a new stadium in neighboring Arlington, Texas. Downtown Dallas is in the background.

125—Parking lots at Los Angeles International Airport, California
LAX occupies 3,425 acres and has nearly 25,000 parking spaces.

165

126—Arizona Mills Mall, Tempe, Arizona
The owner of this mall, The Mills Corporation, is a real estate investment trust (REIT). Today there are about 180 REITs publicly traded on major stock exchanges. Mills owns fifteen malls such as this one, strategically located on the urbanizing periphery, fifteen to forty miles from the city center.

127—Self-storage facility along Interstate Highway 60, Surprise, Arizona   1
The nation's two largest self-storage real estate investment trusts are Public Storage and Shurgard.
Combined, these companies own more than 2,000 self-storage facilities in forty states and eighty
U.S. cities. They offer over 110 million square feet of rentable space.

169

Waste Landscapes of Infrastructure (LINs)

The compulsory landscaping had yet to be carried out by the contractors, and the original contents of this shabby tract, its rusting cars and course grass, were still untouched.
–J.G. Ballard, *Concrete Island*

Infrastructure is ubiquitous throughout all urbanized landscapes. Cities, regardless of location or size, require a variety of infrastructural systems in order to function. Waste landscapes of infrastructure (LINs) include the landscape surfaces associated with these systems, including easements, setbacks, and rights-of-way associated with transportation (such as highway corridors and interchanges), electric transmissions (see figures 128, 129), oil and gas pipelines, waterways, and railways. As the technology for communications, energy, and transportation evolve or change, these LINs expand and contract, which inevitably results in jurisdiction transfers from public to private uses and vice versa.

In the U.S. there are nearly 4 million miles of paved and unpaved roads.[12] The National Highway System, now more than 160,000 miles long, carries 1 trillion, or 45 percent, of the vehicle miles traveled by trucks and passenger vehicles.[13] There are more than 590,000 bridges associated with the network of U.S. highway intersections, ramps, and crossings.[14] Roadside "landscaped" corridors, medians, and adjacent rights-of-way add roughly 42,200 square miles of land surface associated with public roads or road corridors in the U.S. (see figures 130, 131, 132).[15]

The number of electronically tolled private highways, built to bypass central, congested traffic areas in order to serve wealthier communities on the urbanizing periphery, is increasing. Rights-of-way for these private toll roads tend to be wider than their publicly owned counterparts, because land is typically cheaper on the urban periphery. Tollway subscribers pay premiums for less traffic congestion. Entry and exit points are planned to control excess tollway traffic flow and facilitate continuous movement. Colorado's privately funded forty-seven-mile toll Beltway, E-470, connects through the newest, most rapidly growing communities on the periphery of Denver.[16]

Table 4

U.S. transportation and energy infrastructure
Landscape statistics

Petroleum-product pipeline	152,000 miles
Natural-gas transport	340,000 miles
High-voltage electrical-transmission lines	154,503 miles
Electrical-transmission lines constructed annually	1,000 miles
Railways, rail yards, and parallel lines	178,000 miles
U.S. National Highway System	160,000 miles
Waterways used for commerce	12,000 miles
Airport locations	19,500

[12] U.S. Department of Transportation, Bureau of Transportation Statistics, North American Transportation Highlights BTS99-07, Washington, DC, December 1999.
[13] "The Role of the National Highway System Connectors: Industry Context and Issues," U.S. Department of Transportation Federal Highway Administration, prepared by A. Strauss-Wieder, Inc. and KPMG Peat Marwick LLP, Louis Berger & Associates, Parsons Brinkerhoff, February, 1999.
[14] U.S. Department of Transportation, Federal Highway Administration, Office of Bridge Technology, National Bridge Inventory Database, August 14, 2001. Also U.S. Department of Transportation, Bureau of Transportation Statistics, North American Transportation Highlights BTS99-07, Table 1–27: Condition of U.S. Highway Bridges, Washington, DC, December 1999.
[15] Forman, *Roadside Ecology*, 44. Author converted Forman's estimate of 27 million acres into square miles.
[16] E-470 Public Highway Authority official web site, http://www.e-470.com.

1

Additional LINs that result from transportation infrastructure roughly include 178,000 miles of land associated with railways, rail yards, and parallel lines.[17] Some 19,500 airports throughout the U.S. contain a variety of paved and grassed surfaces for aviation use.[18] Waterways used for commerce account for 12,000 miles of land and water interfaces.[19]

Infrastructure associated with energy includes extensive networks of crude-oil and natural-gas pipelines and electric transmission-line rights-of-way (see figures 133, 134). There are approximately 152,000 miles of petroleum-product pipeline in the U.S.[20] The natural-gas transportation network includes more than 340,000 miles of pipeline. Rights-of-way for oil and gas pipelines are strips of land, usually about 25 to 150 feet wide. High-voltage electrical-transmission lines occupy more than 154,503 miles. About a thousand miles of electrical-transmission line are built per year in the U.S. (see table 4).[21] As transportation modes and energy production and consumption change in the future, LINs will need to be adaptively redesigned. As linear systems already running between all urbanized areas, LINs have the potential to be reused for socially and ecologically reconnecting increasingly deconcentrated populations.

128

129

130

131

132

133

134

[17] U.S. Department of Transportation, Bureau of Transportation Statistics, North American Transportation Highlights BTS99-07, Washington, DC, December 1999.
[18] Ibid. Table 1–3: Number of U.S. Airport locations.
[19] U.S. Central Intelligence Agency, The World Factbook, http://www.cia.gov/cia/publications/factbook/index.html.
[20] Ibid.
[21] Ibid. Also see U.S. Department of Energy, Electricity Transmission Fact Sheet, http://eia.doe.gov.

128—Electrical transmission line right-of-way, Plano, Texas
As energy transportation infrastructure and technology evolve, transmission line rights-of-way
will be sold and converted into new land uses.

129—Electrical transmission line right-of-way, Charlotte, North Carolina

About a thousand miles of electrical transmission lines are built annually in the U.S.

130—Interchange construction at Interstate Highways 610 / 10, Houston, Texas
The National Highway System, now more than 160,000 miles long, carries 1 trillion or 45 percent
of the vehicle miles traveled by trucks and passenger vehicles. In the U.S., there are nearly 4 million
miles of paved and unpaved roads for vehicular travel.

131—Interchange at Interstate Highways 210 / 15, San Bernardino, California
Roadside "landscaped" corridors, medians, and adjacent rights-of-way results in roughly 42,200
square miles of land surface associated with public roads or road corridors in the U.S.

132—Interchange at Interstate Highways 60 / 10, Phoenix, Arizona
Interstate 60 is an east to west highway running from Virginia to Arizona. It terminates at Interstate 10,
which is the southernmost east to west interstate highway in the U.S.

133—Houston Ship Channel, Texas
Houston Ship Channel is part of the largest U.S. petroleum port. More than 420 petrochemical plants and two of the nation's four biggest oil refineries are in this area.

134—Electrical transmission line right-of-way running through Addicks Reservoir, Houston, Texas.

Waste Landscapes of Obsolescence (LOOs)

Capital creates and destroys its own landscape.
–David Harvey, *The Geopolitics of Capitalism*

Vast quantities of waste are created in the U.S. each year by households, businesses, government, agriculture, mining, and other industries. It comes in solids, liquids, and gases and affects everything, especially our air and water resources. The automobile is an example of waste found throughout areas of urbanization. In addition to the roads and infrastructure needed for automobile use, there are more cars than drivers in the average American household (1.75 drivers and 1.90 personal vehicles).[22] In 2003 more than 12 million automobiles were scrapped or junked (see figures 135, 136).[23]

Waste landscapes of obsolescence (LOOs) refer to sites that are designed for accommodating consumer wastes. These include municipal–solid waste landfills and wastewater-treatment facilities (see figures 137, 138). America's per capita municipal solid waste doubled from 1960 to 1990.[24] Today, however, there are fewer landfills located within central cities. During the 1970s there were roughly 20,000 public and private landfills in the U.S. By the end of the 1980s, 6,000 remained. By 1999 there were only 2,268 landfills. These landfills are operated mostly by private companies, which accommodate all of the municipal solid waste.[25] There are many reasons for the evolution and consolidation of landfills. They stem from regulations and economics that have made the creation of new landfills further from city centers less costly than expanding existing facilities in highly populated areas. By 2000 Browning-Ferris Industries (now called Allied Waste Industries Inc.) and Waste Management Inc. owned more than 2 billion cubic yards of permitted landfill capacity. Combined, they handle two thirds of America's municipal solid waste. Today these two companies own and operate more than 450 active landfill sites and 500 transfer stations (see figures 139, 140). This is enough capacity to dispose of about 160 million tons of waste per year for the next four decades.[26] Similar trends occur with wastewater-treatment facilities, which have increasingly become privatized and consolidated (see figures 141,142).[27]

[22] Matthew L. Wald, "One Vehicle on the Road, Two Others in the Garage," *New York Times*, August 30, 2003, B12.
[23] U.S. Department of Transportation, Bureau of Transportation Statistics, North American Transportation Highlights BTS99-07, Table 4-54: Motor Vehicles Scrapped, Washington, DC, December 1999.
[24] U.S. EPA.
[25] Ibid. There are many reasons for this transformation in municipal solid waste handling. For a summary see Richard C. Porter, *The Economics of Waste* (Washington, DC: Resources for the Future, 2002), 54–55; For a social context see Rathje and Murphy, *Rubbish: The Archeology of Garbage*.
[26] Author's calculations based on 2003–04 data from company prospecti.
[27] See Reason Public Policy Institute (RPPI), "Focus on Water and Wastewater: Privatization Watch," 28. 2 (2004).

135

136

137

138

139

140

141

142

187

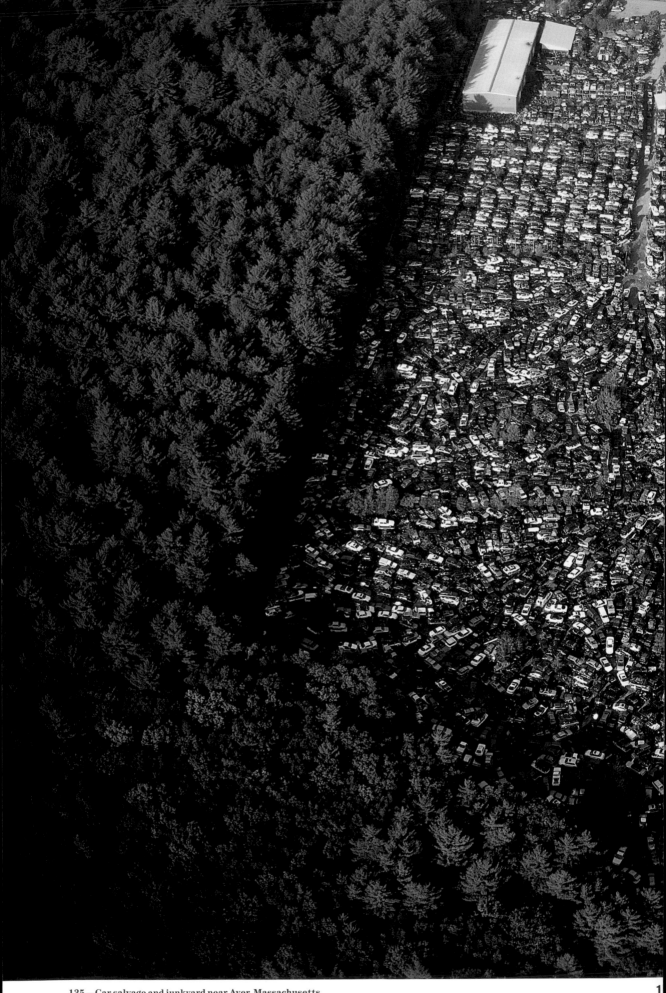

135—Car salvage and junkyard near Ayer, Massachusetts
In 2003, over 12 million automobiles were scrapped or junked in the U.S.

136—Car salvage and junkyards near Dallas, Texas
There are more cars than drivers in the average American household (1.75 drivers and 1.90 personal vehicles).

137—Housing in Riverside, California
In the U.S., municipal solid waste per capita doubled from 1960 to 1990.

138—Landfill in Buford, Georgia
Municipal solid waste landfills are mostly operated by private companies that accommodate all of
the (non-toxic) refuse. Newer landfills are located well outside central cities, where large inexpensive
land masses exist.

139—City of Dallas McCommas Bluff Landfill, Texas
McCommas is the nation's ninth largest landfill with enough capacity to last beyond 2050. The landfill
receives 7,000 tons of waste daily. Downtown Dallas is in the background.

1

140—City of Dallas McCommas Bluff Landfill, Texas
The landfill receives an average waste volume of 1.7 million tons per year. Many private hauling
companies use the landfill, which charges a $15 per ton tipping fee. By 2000, Browning-Ferris Industries
(now called Allied Waste Industries, Inc.) and Waste Management, Inc. owned more than 2 billion

cubic yards of permitted landfill capacity in the U.S. Combined, they handle two-thirds of America's municipal solid waste. Today, these two companies own and operate more than 450 active landfill disposal sites and 500 transfer stations.

141—Metro Wastewater Reclamation Plant, Commerce City, Colorado, five miles north of downtown Denver
Water leaving this facility is dumped into the South Platte River and is used for irrigation, commercial applications, lakes, and wildlife refuges.

142—Central Wastewater Treatment Plant, Trinity River, Dallas, Texas
The City of Dallas Water Utilities is a not-for-profit department providing water and wastewater services to about 1.9 million people in Dallas and twenty-six nearby communities. There are about 6,000 wastewater treatment plants in the U.S., which are increasingly becoming privatized and consolidated.

Waste Landscapes of Exchange (LEXs)

Christmas is a solid-waste tsunami.
–William Rathje and Cullen Murphy,
Rubbish: The Archeology of Garbage

"Demalling," or the vacancy rate of older shopping centers, is increasing across the U.S.[28] As of 2001, more than 440 regional indoor malls, representing 21 percent of all malls, were declared abandoned, dead, or dying (see figure 143).[29] After years of consolidation, the ten largest mall REITs control more than 47 percent of all malls and all of the two hundred high-performing malls. This consolidation favors the gigantic, newly built super-regional malls, or class A malls, which average more than $400 per square foot in tenant sales (see figures 144, 145, 146, 147). Class B and C malls, or older, midsize developments with sales well below $400 per square foot, are inferior to their A counterparts. Weaker sales are thought to be the result of competitive disadvantages, such as bad location, poor infrastructure, or vacant tenant space.[30] These variables are compounded by demographic shifts, such as the erosion of customer bases in older parts of cities as people move to newer, peripheral locations.

Aging regional and smaller malls are squeezed out of the marketplace from two sides of the retail spectrum. On one side are the newer, bigger malls that incorporate service-driven anchor retailers (Nordstrom, Bloomingdale's, etc.), entertainment, themed environments, restaurants, and other sellers of luxury goods. These retail environments achieve high tenant sale revenues per square foot by selling goods at full retail premiums. On the other side are the big-box retailers and discounters (Costco, Sam's Club, Wal-Mart, Target, etc.) that mostly sell lower-cost, non-luxury items but at higher volumes (see figures 148, 149). These retailers offer customers superior access with new road infrastructure and large parking lots. As the horizontal city expands, so do both of these types of retail environments.

There is an abundance of abandoned, vacant, and decaying malls and retail centers, which were once the main shopping venues in their respective cities. The hundreds of older retail malls left behind by this new wave of development exemplify waste landscapes of exchange (LEXs). LEXs are not limited solely to mall-type retail. Relatively new big-box retailers are replacing their smaller stores with "supercenters" leaving empty, vacant, or abandoned property and buildings scattered across the country. Wal-Mart closed nearly three hundred stores in recent years in the effort

[28] Peter Hochstein and Morris Newman, "The Art of Demalling," *Retail Traffic Magazine*, http://retailtrafficmag.com/mag/retail_art_demalling/ (accessed May 1, 2003).

[29] This according to a 2001 study by Pricewaterhouse Coopers and the Congress for the New Urbanism.

[30] Kenneth Rogers, "Look Out Below!" *Retail Traffic Magazine*, http://retailtrafficmag.com/retailing/propmgmt/retail_look_below/ (accessed August 1, 2003).

to consolidate its retail operations into supercenters.[31]
During the past five years Montgomery Ward, JCPenney,
Stern's, Kmart, Sears, and Lord & Taylor, among
others, closed more than seven hundred stores that
were considered anchors in regional and smaller
retail malls as part of bankruptcies, restructurings,
or market repositioning.[32]

143

144

145

146

147

148

149

[31] Eric M. Weiss, "Big-Box Stores Leave More Than a Void," *Washington
Post*, January 20, 2004, B01.
[32] Curt Hazlett, "The Replacements," *Retail Traffic Magazine*,
http://retailtrafficmag.com/development/trends/retail_replacements/
index.html (accessed October 1, 2003).

143—Northwest Mall, Houston, Texas

One of Houston's many aging malls, Northwest is six miles from downtown. As of 2001 over 440 indoor regional malls, representing 21 percent of all U.S. malls, were declared abandoned, dead, or dying.

144—Desert Ridge Marketplace, Scottsdale, Arizona, about twenty-five miles north of Phoenix
This Class A, super-regional mall is part of the Desert Ridge master-planned community, a development covering 5,700 acres, which broke ground in 1997. This new mall has 1.3 million square feet of retail and entertainment space.

145—Stonebriar Centre Mall, Frisco, Texas, about thirty miles north of Dallas
Stonebriar spans 1.7 million square feet of retail space including a NHL-sized ice rink and a 24-screen
AMC theatre. It is the largest Class A, or super-regional mall, in North Texas. Its surrounding population
has grown over 400 percent over the past ten years.

146—The Mall of Georgia, Gwinnett County, Georgia, about thirty miles northeast of Atlanta
This Class A, super-regional mall is the second largest mall in the southeast, occupying 2.2 million square feet on 180 acres of a total 550-acre tract. It has over 9,000 parking spaces.

147—Irvine Spectrum Center, Irvine, California
Its 1.6 million square feet includes a 21-screen theater complex and a 6.5-story, stadium-style IMAX theater.

148—Big Box retailers between Denver and Boulder along Highway 36, Colorado
Big box retailers are replacing their smaller stores with "supercenters" leaving empty, vacant,
or abandoned property and buildings scattered across the U.S. Wal-Mart closed nearly three hundred
of its smaller stores in recent years in an effort to consolidate its retail operations into supercenters.

149—New strip mall road infrastructure in Surprise, Arizona, about twenty miles from Phoenix
Big box retailers and discounters (Costco, Sam's Club, Wal-Mart, Target, etc.) offer customers superior
access through new road infrastructure and expansive parking lots.

Waste Landscapes of Contamination (LOCOs)

Some asked why we're proposing any base closures during a time of war.
The answer is the changes are essential in helping us win this conflict.
–Donald Rumsfeld, *Secretary of the U.S. Department of Defense*
(May 16, 2005)

Waste landscapes of contamination (LOCOs) include
such public and federal installations as airports, military
bases, ammunition depots and training grounds, and
sites used for mining and petroleum and chemical
operations (see figures 150, 151). Since the 1990s, local,
state, and federal agencies have sought to reinvest
LOCOs into more profitable and appropriate uses as
urbanization has spread closer to their borders. Many
sites have experienced degrees of contamination
as a result of their previous land use; they must be
reclaimed or decontaminated prior to redevelopment.
Deindustrialization creates a wealth of former industrial
landscapes within older portions of U.S. cities (see
chapter 3). LOCOs are sometimes visually difficult to
detect. Contamination may appear from underground
sources, spread as subterranean plumes in groundwater
and soil, and then settle. Invisible to the naked eye,
plumes require chemical analysis, core sampling,
and sophisticated computer modeling for detection
(see figures 152, 153).
     The National Priorities List (Superfund) and
Brownfields are two distinct programs created by
the federal government to respectively reclaim
and redevelop LOCOs. There are nearly 1,300 sites
still awaiting Superfund cleanup and reclamation.
Many are in urbanized areas. Since the early 1990s,
three waves of military-base closings have resulted
in the sale and conversion of more than a hundred
thousand acres of federal land (and thousands of
buildings) to private redevelopment.[33] In addition,
dozens of regional, municipal, and other small airports
throughout the U.S. face redevelopment as the result
of encroaching urbanization, increased land values,
and the desire for noise abatement by new residents
(see figures 154, 155). LOCOs often present designers
of the built environment with complex (and potentially
lethal) situations that require a new, complex blend
of knowledge and skills ranging from biological and
physical sciences to law and economics.

[33]U.S. Department of Defense.

2

150

151

152

153

154

155

150—Ammunition bunkers at Ravenna Arsenal, Portage County between Ravenna and Warren, Ohio
The arsenal produced and stored artillery and mortar shells for World War II and the Korean and Vietnam
wars. In 1992 the site was decommissioned. More than 95 percent of the 21,419 acres was transferred to
the Ohio National Guard for training in 1998. The site has proven contamination of the land and buildings.

151—Ammunition assembly line structures at Ravenna Arsenal, Portage County between Ravenna and Warren, Ohio   **22**
Since the early 1990s three waves of military base closings have resulted in the decommissioning of ninety-seven facilities, including nineteen active and inactive ammunitions plants. This resulted in the sale and conversion of more than 100,000 acres of federal land (and thousands of buildings) to private redevelopment.

152—Papago Military Reservation, Phoenix / Scottsdale, Arizona
Papago contains a military museum and a facility used by the Arizona National Guard. It is bordered by
residential housing and, to the southwest, by the ninety-acre Motorola semiconductor products plant,
which has known contamination and Superfund status.

153—Joliet Arsenal, Joliet, Illinois, about forty-five miles southwest of Chicago
Most of the 1,462 buildings on the Arsenal are still standing, although idle for more than twenty
years. During World War II, the Arsenal had 200 miles of road, 166 miles of railroad, and 392
munitions bunkers (in the foreground), many of which will be left as is. The Arsenal, surrounded

by thirty-seven miles of eight-foot barbed-wire fence, is being converted into the Midewin National
Tallgrass Prairie. A new intermodal facility abuts the property.

154—Dallas Naval Air Station, Texas
This 833-acre base was decommissioned in 1993. New housing development abuts the lakefront property.
Downtown Dallas is in the background.

155—Burke Lakefront Airport, Cleveland, Ohio
The airport sits on top of a former garbage dump. Soil and water beneath the runway are believed to
contain contamination. The runways and other paved areas provide a cap for the site until further testing
or remediation begins.

Part Three
The Drosscape Manifesto

Chaptor Five
Drosscape Explained

All world's glory is but dross unclean.
–Edmund Spenser *(1595)*

Drosscape Defined

Thus far this book has focused on the waste landscapes of urban America, along with the processes that are contributing to their formation. This last chapter introduces drosscape, a term created to describe a design pedagogy that emphasizes the productive integration and reuse of waste landscapes throughout the urban world.

Planning and design cannot solve all problems associated with the vast amount of urban waste landscape (see figure 156). However, the alarm s sounded to those who cope with the increased pessimism and cynicism spawned by the inefficacy of the "big four" design disciplines (landscape architecture, urban design, planning, and architecture) in the face of unfettered, market-driven development. The recent emergence of landscape urbanism may be a reaction to the frustration shared by many people in the landscape, planning, and architectural design arenas.[1] The polarizing rhetorical arguments of the pro- and anti- urbanization contingencies, as well as dynamic economic processes make traditional masterplanning approaches for future cities seem absurd. But advocating a revolutionary form of urban landscape study and practice, such as landscape urbanism, is *not* exclusive of the big four design disciplines. There is no need to develop an entirely new design discipline in order to rethink landscape's relationship to urbanization. Drosscape has the potential to coexist with the big four design disciplines. By working within current educational and professional practices, designers can still promote a radically different outcome.

The term *drosscape* implies that dross, or waste, is scaped, or resurfaced, and reprogrammed by human intentions. Moreover, the ideas of dross and scape have individual attributes.[2] The use of the term *dross* in this chapter builds on Lars Lerup's use of the term (see chapter 1) but departs from Lerupian origin in scope and value. The suggestive etymology of the word includes shared origins with the words *waste* and *vast*, two terms frequently used to describe the contemporary nature of horizontal urbanization, as well as connections to the words *vanity*, *vain*, *vanish*, and *vacant*, all of which relate to waste through the form of empty gestures (see figure 157).[3]

Both dross and scape are created and destroyed by processes and values derived from, or because of cultural tastes and actions. Drosscape is the creation of a new condition in which vast, wasted, or wasteful

[1] Charles Waldheim, ed., *Landscape Urbanism: A Reference Manifesto* (New York: Princeton Architectural Press, 2006). Dean J. Almy III and Michael Benedikt, eds., *CENTER 14: Landscape Urbanism* (Austin, Texas: Center for American Architecture and Design, 2006).
[2] I discuss a similar position for the term *reclaiming landscape*, of "land" and "scape" in *Reclaiming the American West*.
[3] *American Heritage Dictionary*.

land surfaces (such as those described in previous chapters) are modeled in accordance with new programs or new sets of values that remove or replace real or perceived wasteful aspects of geographical space (i.e., redevelopment, toxic waste removal, tax revenues, etc.). Drosscaping, as a verb, is the placement upon the landscape of new social programs that transform waste (real or perceived) into more productive urbanized landscapes to some degree (see figure 158).

Drosscape demands a strategically phased implementation of design that other "clean," or "green" types of urbanization lack because they are not immediately wholly occupiable.[4] Sites formerly containing industrial or manufacturing facilities, for instance, have soil, water, and building contamination problems left over from chemicals and hazardous materials. This condition, and all of the others described in this book, presents a novel set of challenges for landscape, infrastructure, and building design professions, which must face the spatio-temporary dimensions of redevelopment as a site is decontaminated, re-regulated, or otherwise transformed for reuse over time.

[4] Sandra Alker, Victoria Joy, Peter Roberts, Nathan Smith, "The Definition of Brownfield," *Journal of Environmental Planning and Management*, vol. 43, no. 11, (London: Routledge, January 2000), 49–69. Note the temporal aspects of the definition of a brownfield by this academic journal: "A Brownfield site is any land or premises which has previously been used or developed and is not currently fully in use, although it may be partially occupied or utilized. It may also be vacant, derelict or contaminated. Therefore a Brownfield site is not necessarily available for immediate use without intervention." Also see Niall Kirkwood, "Here Come the Hyper-accumulators!" *Harvard Design Magazine* 17, Fall 2002/Winter 2003, 52–56.

Previous spread—*War of the Worlds* movie set, Universal Studios, Hollywood, California
Waste is valued for tourism as long as it makes a profit. A dismantled Boeing 747 lies in the landscape as part of the back-lot studio tram tour (seen on the roads). The cost of the tour starts at $51 per person.

156—Commercial corridor redevelopment at Beltway 8 and Interstate Highway 10 (Katy Freeway) in Houston, Texas
Drosscape is the creation of a new condition in which "vast," "waste," or "wasteful" land surfaces are modeled in accordance with new programs or new sets of values that remove or replace real or perceived wasteful aspects of geographical space (i.e. redevelopment, toxic waste removal, tax revenues, etc.).

Dispersal Graph Comparison
Population density and distance from city center
in ten U.S. metropolitan regions.

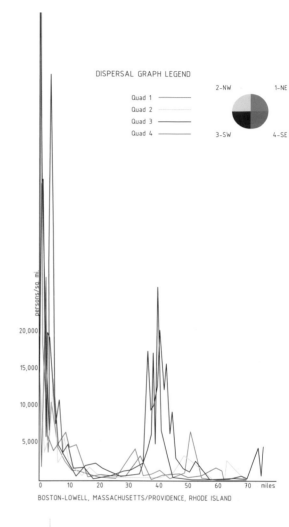

DISPERSAL GRAPH LEGEND

Quad 1 —————
Quad 2 —————
Quad 3 —————
Quad 4 —————

2-NW   1-NE

3-SW   4-SE

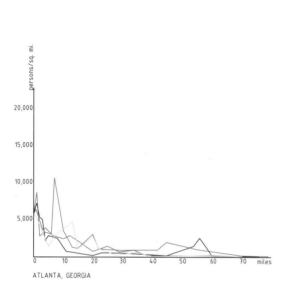

ATLANTA, GEORGIA

BOSTON-LOWELL, MASSACHUSETTS/PROVIDENCE, RHODE ISLAND

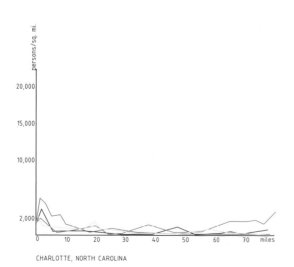

CHARLOTTE, NORTH CAROLINA

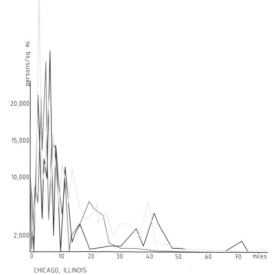

CHICAGO, ILLINOIS

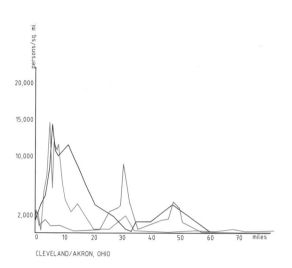

CLEVELAND/AKRON, OHIO

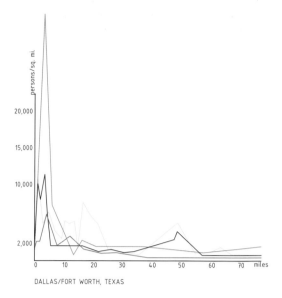

DALLAS/FORT WORTH, TEXAS

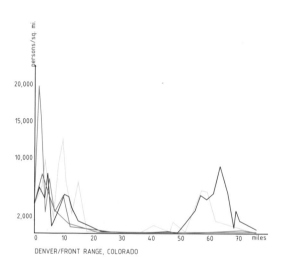

DENVER/FRONT RANGE, COLORADO

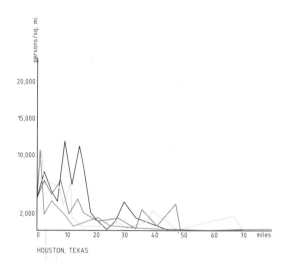

HOUSTON, TEXAS

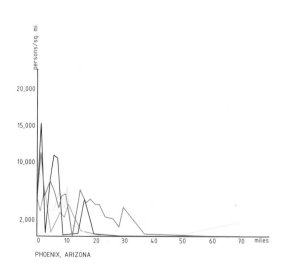

PHOENIX, ARIZONA

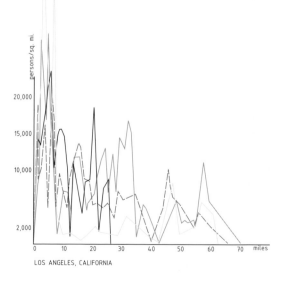

LOS ANGELES, CALIFORNIA

Spindle Chart Comparison

Manufacturing decline and growth, and distance from city center, compared in ten U.S. metropolitan regions.

SPINDLE CHARTS LEGEND

Change In Manufacturing Establishments + Distance From Center

Manufacturing Establishments Change, 1977–1992
Manufacturing Establishments Growth, 1992–2001
Manufacturing Establishments Decline, 1992–2001

70 miles
40 miles
10 miles

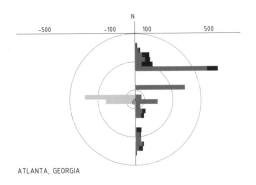

ATLANTA, GEORGIA

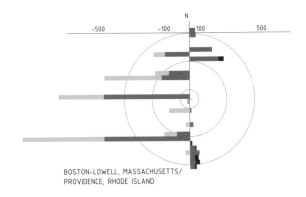

BOSTON-LOWELL, MASSACHUSETTS/
PROVIDENCE, RHODE ISLAND

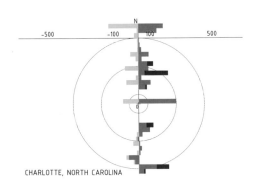

CHARLOTTE, NORTH CAROLINA

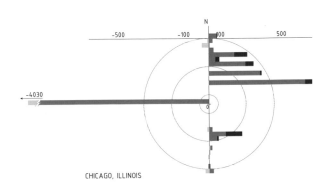

CHICAGO, ILLINOIS

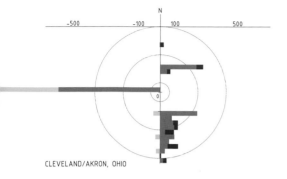

CLEVELAND/AKRON, OHIO

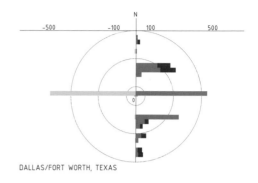

DALLAS/FORT WORTH, TEXAS

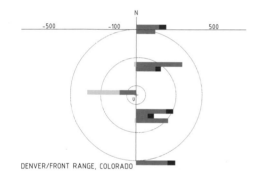

DENVER/FRONT RANGE, COLORADO

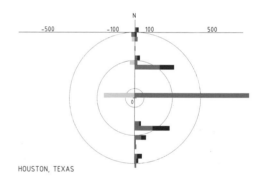

HOUSTON, TEXAS

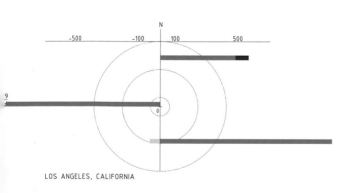

LOS ANGELES, CALIFORNIA

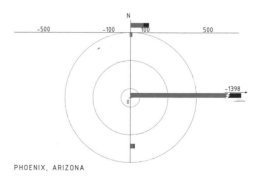

PHOENIX, ARIZONA

Figure and Caption Sources

Figure 1. Urban Land Surfaces in the U.S.
U.S. Census Bureau, Statistical Abstract of the United States: 2003, and population characteristics: 1900–2002 at http://www.census.gov/prod/www/abs/statab.html (accessed June 10, 2004); Ralph E. Heimlich and William D. Anderson, *Development at the Urban Fringe and Beyond: Impacts on Agriculture and Rural Land*, Agricultural Economic Report No. AER803 (Washington, D.C.: Resource Economics Division, Economic Research Service, USDA, June, 2001), http://www.ers.usda.gov/publications/aer803/ (accessed April 20, 2004). For further classifications of "urbanized area" from the Census Bureau, see http://www.census.gov/population/www/estimates/metroarea.html (accessed June 14, 2005).

Figure 2. Landscape Urbanization in the U.S.
U.S. Census Bureau, Statistical Abstract of the United States: 2003, Table 2 Population, Housing Units, Area Measurements, and Density: 1790–1990 and Table 4 Population: 1790–1990 at http://www.census.gov/population/www/censusdata/hiscendata.html (accessed June 10, 2004).

Figure 19. Manufacturing Productivity in the U.S.
U.S. Census Bureau, Economic Census Data for Counties, 1977–92 at http:// censtats.census.gov/usa/usa.shtml (accessed June 11, 2004), and 2001 Economic Census Data, County Business Patterns Economic Profile at http://quickfacts.census.gov/qfd (accessed June 11, 2004). Data collected for the counties surrounding fifteen major U.S. cities, U.S. Department of Commerce, Bureau of Economic Analysis Tables 6.4 A–C; Full-Time and Part-Time Employees by Industry; Current-dollar and real GDP at http://www.bea.doc.gov/. U.S. Bureau of Labor Statistics: Table 1 Manufacturing: Productivity and Related Indexes, 1949–2001: Productivity Output Per Hour of All Persons at http://stats.bls.gov/lpc/home.htm#data (accessed June 12, 2004).

Figure 21. Urban Land Density in the U.S.
See sources for figure 1.

Figure 40. Urban Land Contamination in the U.S.

Figure 51. Landscape Contamination in the U.S.
U.S. EPA official web site for brownfields, http://www.epa.gov/brownfields; U.S. EPA official web site for Superfund, http://www.epa.gov/superfund; U.S. EPA official web site for Toxic Release Inventory, http://www.epa.gov/tri/ (all accessed July 20, 2004).

Figure 41. Dina Cappiello, "In Harm's Way,"
Houston Chronicle January 17, 2005, A-1, 12-15. See http://chron.com/toxics (accessed January 17, 2005).

Figures 54 through 114. All Population, Housing, and Business Statistics from U.S. Bureau of the Census; For figure 54 see Logistics Facilities Group, Colliers International, http://www.logfac.com (accessed June 14, 2005).

Figure 58. Dekalb-Peachtree Airport official web site. See http://www.pdkairport.org/economic.htm (accessed May 4, 2005).

Figure 66. Raleigh, North Carolina's official city economic development web site. See http://www.raliegh4u.com/economy_demographics/ (accessed April 20, 2005).

Figure 68. North Carolina State Demographics official web site. See http://demog.state.nc.us/ (accessed June 1, 2005).

Figure 70. Kannapolis, North Carolina's official city web site. See http://www.ci.kannapolis.nc.us/media_8.asp (accessed June 14, 2005).

Figure 72. Southeast Environmental Taskforce (SETF) official web site. See http://www.southeastenvironmental.org/open.html (accessed June 3, 2005).

Figure 91. Total Maximum Daily Load Program (TMDL) case study, "Denver Metro: The South Platte River Segment EPA841-F-93-001," U.S. EPA Office of Water official web site. See http://www.epa.gov/OWOW/TMDL/cs1/cs1.htm (accessed June 2, 2005).

Figure 95. Rocky Mountain Steel Mills, a division of Oregon Steel Mills official web site. See http://www.oregonsteel.com/RMSM/rmsmpg3.htm (accessed June 1, 2005).

Figure 97. New release, "Union Pacific Honored for Excellence by the Newcomer Society Houston," official web site of Union Pacific Railroad, June, 25 2002. See http://www.uprr.com/notes/corpcomm/2002/020625_newcomen.shtml (accessed June 25, 2002).

Figure 102. Texas Medical Center official web site, facts and figures page, 2005. See http://www.tmc.edu/tmc-facts.html (accessed June 14, 2005).

Figure 105. Rancho Cucamonga, California's official city web site. See http://www.ci.rancho-cucamonga.ca.us/index_res.htm (accessed June 14, 2005).

Figure 111. Carol E. Heim, "Leapfrogging, Urban Sprawl, and Growth Management: Phoenix, 1950–2000," *The American Journal of Economics and Sociology (AJES)*, (Oxford: Blackwell, January 2001); News release, "BNSF Logistics, LLC. and Autolog Corporation Announce the Initiation of a New Auto Transport (Car-Rail) Service Geared Toward the Needs of Snowbirds," Burlington Northern Santa Fe Corporation (BNSF Logistics) official web site. See http://www.bnsflogistics.com/jan122004.asp (accessed January 12, 2004).

Figure 113. Maricopa Association of Governments; IMPLAN, January 2005 (original source), Greater Phoenix Economic Council official web site. See http://www.gpec.org/InfoCenter/Topics/Industry_Clusters/High-Tech.html (accessed January 14, 2004).